M000317131

How to Write Your Novel in Nine Weeks

BILL DODDS

—with—

LITTLE WILLIE SOCKSPEARE

Copyright © 2019 Bill Dodds

All rights reserved.

ISBN-10: 0-9840908-9-4
ISBN-13: 978-0-9840908-9-1

What reviewers are saying about
How to Write Your Novel in Nine Weeks

"Not academic, not self-righteous or pompous, this book is like taking a new friend along while writing, writing, writing every day. Witty encouragement from an already published author and teacher."

"I found this book inspiring and amusing. Writers needing a jump start would find this useful. Just the right amount of advice. Thank you, Bill."

"A humorous easy-to-read book that cuts through the hype and encourages novel writing. I enjoyed the witty writing and am now very seriously considering picking up my abandoned draft and resuming the writing process."

"Bill Dodds, and his alter ego Little Willie Sockspeare, have written the most helpful, most fun book ever on how to write a novel — in nine weeks or otherwise. Discouraged? Frustrated? Afraid? Worry not. This book is the answer to all your reservations."

"Writing a novel is tough. You start with great enthusiasm. But that enthusiasm is fragile, and quickly wanes. This book is for everyone who would love to write a novel, whether they've tried before and failed, or been too scared to write the first words."

.

CONTENTS

Week Zero

Week Three

Week Four

Week Five

Appendix: Sample Chapters

(More Lies) About the Author

Dedication

For all novelists-to-be.
You can do it!
Really.
And especially for (<u>insert your name here</u>).
You're my favorite.

1
WEEK ZERO

Week ... *What?*

"Wait a minute!" you may be saying to yourself. "This book is how to write a book in *nine* weeks and if you start with 'Week Zero' and go to 'Week Nine,' isn't that really *ten* weeks?"

Perhaps.

When Week One begins—and I could start it right now, you know, so don't get too huffy—you're going to be writing from Day 1.

Not outlining.

Not researching.

Not telling yourself or others how you have this novel "in your head" and all you have to do now is "write it down."

No way! On Week One, Day 1 you put your pen in your hand or your fingers on your keyboard and you *write*.

"Oh, yeah?" you might be saying now. "Well, what if I have one of those software programs and I just talk into the computer microphone and my words appear on the screen and ... ."

To which I reply: "You're not in the seventh grade and I'm not your substitute teacher." You can speak, type, write, print, chisel ... But here's the bottom line: If you want to have a novel completed by the end of Week Nine, Day 6, you're going to be writing on Week One, Day 1.

Preparing for Week One, Day 1

So, how do you get ready for that fateful first day? You make a rough outline by:

1. Deciding what kind of a novel you want to write. Your genre.

2. Considering a plot.

3. Picking a setting.

4. Coming up with a few characters you like ... or hate ... and giving them some obstacles to deal with.

Jot it all down and realize that once you start the actual writing, each and every one of those might go right out the window.

Be honest: You already have a lot of those in mind, don't you? Of course you do. You've been thinking about them for a long, long time.

5. One final point. You may find it helpful to skim through the book before you begin your nine-week trek. Each chapter has a tip to be looked at, considered ... and possibly rejected.

A Simple Plan

This nine-week method is based on a daily word count. I don't care if it takes you only five minutes to reach it. I don't care if it takes three hours. Word count is what matters. The number of words you write that day on your novel is all that matters. (Not all that matters in your whole life or in the whole world, but you know what I mean.)

I'll start you off easy.

Week One: 300 words per day for six days. (Take the seventh day off. You'll have completed 1,800 words. Good

2

for you!)

Week Two: 400 words per day for six days. (And another day off. Now you'll be up to 4,200 words.)

Weeks Three through Nine: 500 words six days a week and that seventh day off.

At this pace and rate your novel will be just over 25,000 words.

And you have two questions, don't you?

1. What's a "Word"?

A word is a word is a word. Long or short. No matter. Yes, there's the theory that one should count the letters in a piece and divide that number by five. *Bah!* You don't have to do that. If you're using a computer, just use the word count. If you're writing on paper, count each word and shout "halleluiah" when you get past your daily quota.

A word-count method works much better than a time requirement. (No doodling on the paper or dawdling on the Internet and calling it "writing.")

And it works better than a page-count system. When I tried that method I soon discovered I could quickly fill two pages with dialogue.

"What?" John asked
"What do you mean what?" Marcia answered.
"I guess I mean 'yes.'"
"So, what you're saying is 'yes'?"
"Yes."

And so on. (An argument worked even better: "Yes." "No." "Yes!" "No!")

On the other hand, a word-count shows no mercy.

2. Will My Book Really Be a "Novel"?

"Mmmm, well, yesssss," you may be willing to grudgingly admit, "all that may be true but 25,000 words isn't a novel. It's a *novella*." (You're thinking this if you majored in English in college. If you majored in math, you're thinking "My book will be 25,200 words.")

So let's dispel the stigma of the "small novel." A novel has no set size. Those who decided a short story is less than this many words, a novella is less than that many words, and a *real* novel has to be at least … . Just made that up. It's not in the Constitution, Ten Commandments, or any law code.

This is especially so in an age when—much to the dismay of publishers—writers are putting their e-books and paperbacks on the Internet, selling them there, and eliminating the publishers.

Let's try a little comparison. (Or an analogy, if you were an English major.)

I'm going to build a house and you're going to build a house. My structure has two stories, a full basement, a bath and a half, three bedrooms, and bay windows. Yours is an A-frame with an open-style main floor and a loft. You *do* have one of those metal spiraling staircases leading up to the loft which, I admit, is nice.

Is your structure a "housella"? No. It's a house. If it's by a lake you might refer to it as a cabin. If it's in the mountains you could say it's a chalet. It can be a cabin-style house. Or a chalet-style house. But it's a *house*.

Still not convinced a 25,000-word manuscript "counts" as a real novel?

Novel or novella? *Animal Farm* by George Orwell. *Of Mice and Men* by John Steinbeck. *The Shawshank Redemption* by Stephen King. Who cares? Each is a great story and that's what matters. Tell a great story. That's what you've been wanting to do and that's what you *can* do.

I can't speak for Orwell, Steinbeck, or King—well, I suppose I could but I might get sued—but I can tell you I wrote a novel of just under 30,000 words and I'm sure it's a novel. *O Father: A Murder Mystery* won the 3-Day Novel Contest in 1990 and was published the following year. As a novel.

I mention it here because I want you to buy a copy of it

on Amazon. [Note to self: Better not be so honest. Really, Bill, what are you thinking?]

I mention it here because I'll be using it as an example throughout this book because I want you to buy a copy of it on Amazon. [Note to self: See previous note to self.]

I mention it here because, as the contest rules demanded, I cranked it out in three days. Really. Over the Labor Day weekend of 1990. Or, over the "Labour" Day weekend of 1990 since the contest was sponsored by a Canadian publisher. I was the first American to win it.

What you're going to do over nine weeks is ... . No, not win a contest but write a *complete novel*. Beginning, middle, end. (Began a lot of beginnings over the years, have you?) After those nine weeks (and that completed novel), it will be easier for you to write another novel but "easier" is a relative word.

Writing a novel is always hard work, whether it takes you three days, nine weeks, many months, or a lot of years. Three days would be a little hectic for you. It was for me and *O Father* wasn't the first novel I'd written. I began two in college and completed each after I graduated. Then I churned out some more of them. None were long, which brings us back to:

The Advantages of Writing a Short Novel

1. The only way to become a novelist is to write a novel.

2. The only way to learn how to write a novel is to write a novel.

3. A short novel can take a lot less time to write than a long novel.

4. A short novel and a long novel contain the same basic elements and demand the same basic skills.

5. It's much easier to complete a long novel if you've already completed a short novel.

6. It's much easier to abandon an attempt at a long novel if you've never completed a short novel. Or never

completed any novel.

The Secret to Writing a Novel

The secret to writing a novel is there is no secret.

You write a novel by writing.

You get better at writing novels by writing more novels.

You can use a method to get from the beginning to the end (which is what this book is about) but any method only offers a structure for you to write. And keep writing. Until the book is done.

When you get done and you look at your manuscript objectively, you may decide, "I wrote one terrible novel. This novel really stinks."

And it very well may. But you wrote a novel and by writing it you began to seriously learn how to write novels. You abandoned the comfortable, theoretical world of "writing a novel" and entered the uncomfortable, real world of "novel writing."

Odds are the first time you baked a loaf of bread it was a disaster. And the first time you took a swing at a golf ball you may have missed the ball and tee completely. If you got better at either it's because you didn't retreat into the world of the theoretical (only reading recipes or only watching pro golfers on TV) but got back in the kitchen and back on the links and ...

made a horrible batch of biscuits or shot an absolutely embarrassing round of golf. Until ...

you learned ... by doing.

What you're doing now isn't just writing a novel but also learning how to write a novel.

About the Author and Coauthor

This really should be a separate major section but if I made it one you'd skip right over it, wouldn't you? I've been writing professionally since the days of carbon paper. Fiction and non-fiction. Books for kids and adults. National columns and articles. Poems and plays. I've had a couple dozen books published by publishers. And a few I've published myself. (You can find out more on all that at BillDodds.com.)

My coauthor, Little Willie Sockspeare, is a sock puppet with a horrible (and inconsistent) British accent who claims to be the author of all Shakespeare's plays. He "helped" with this book because:

1. Forcing you to read or hear only me day after day seemed a little bleak.

2. Creating an alter ego made this more entertaining for me which, it would follow, should make it more entertaining for you.

3. I have a screw loose, as do you or you wouldn't even consider writing a novel. (Write your novel and it will get looser.)

To hear a podcast of the coauthors discussing all this, visit:

https://archive.org/details/HowToWriteYourNovelInNine Weeks

2
WEEK ONE, DAY 1

BD: Begin by Beginning

Today you're going to write the first 300 words of your novel which may not end up being the first 300 words of your novel.

What do I mean? A few weeks from now you may write part of a chapter and decide, "*This* should be how the book begins!" And you'll do a little editing and revising.

As a journalist and columnist, I've learned it isn't unusual for the "lede"—the opening paragraph—to pop up a few paragraphs into a piece. As a novelist, I know sometimes Chapter 1 hides in part of Chapter 3 or 4 and has to be plopped down where it belongs.

But to start at all, you have to start *somewhere*. You have to move from the "it's in my head" or "it's *all* in my head" to something written on paper or hard drive or papyrus or ... but you get the point.

Week One, Day 1 brings two dangers. The first is you're frozen with fear, doubt, grim memories of past attempts, and so on. You're concerned, or truly believe, you won't be able to write anything. Or at least, not something good.

Who said anything about writing something *good*? No one used *that* G-word. Today's G-word is "goal." Your goal is 300 words. If you write that amount you've had a successful day and you're off to a great start. But ... .

The second danger of Week One, Day 1 is you'll get into the swing of this and want to blow right by that number limit. You'll want to crank out 500, 600, 700 words.

Don't.

Slow and steady wins the race. The tortoise and the hare. This is a marathon not a sprint. Pick any cliché you like. The very real danger is if you go beyond 300 today you will have nothing left in the tank for tomorrow. It's a wonderful feeling to be done with a day's writing and know you have more you not only *want* to write but *can* write.

Do I mean you have to hit exactly 300 words today? No. I mean reach 300 and finish that sentence or paragraph. Then print it out, back it up, and be on your merry way.

3
WEEK ONE, DAY 2

LWS: How to More Easily Start Each Day's Writing

Little Willie here.

Bill, God bless his simple soul, has a few ideas but let's be honest. He wrote a children's poem titled "Mrs. Stein." I dashed off *Hamlet.* Enough said.

Best to have each of us contributing to this book with his own perspective and experience.

Today you're beginning the day after your beginning. That can be a wee bit tough. I remember when I penned "Two households, both alike in dignity/In fair Verona, where we lay our scene" and then "steak and kidney pie" popped into my head and, well, that was that. After lunch and a nap I deemed it too late to continue that day and so I opted for "to-morrow and to-morrow and to-morrow." Only, alas, when tomorrow came I had no idea where I was going with that Verona business.

I mean I had a general outline from "boy-meets-girl to (*spoiler alert!*) boy-poisons-self and girl-stabs-self," but what came immediately after "where we lay our scene"?

Dashed if I knew! Not to mention this Verona business.

Italy? Seriously?

What I discovered, after many days like that, is to jot down a note or two on what I wanted to write tomorrow. For example: "Finish opening sonnet. Star-cross'd lovers. Their deaths bring end to houses' strife. Tip of the hat to audience members."

On the other hand, if I quit for the day right after finishing a scene (or worse, an act), I felt as if I had used up all my creative juices the day before and remained spent. (In today's popular vernacular, I was trying to run on fumes.)

Here the solution was to go a bit farther into what came next. In your case, it means this: Don't stop for the day at the end of the scene or end of the chapter. Write a few sentences of the next scene. Write a few lines of the next chapter.

And then jot down a couple of notes for what comes next.

You'll save yourself a lot of toil and trouble.

4
WEEK ONE, DAY 3

BD: The Myth of the Muses

Let's get a little theological today. In the past, if you've been waiting for the Muses—in Greek mythology the goddesses that inspire creativity—you've been doomed to failure.

Yes, there well may be a spark within you that says "Write!" but ... the Lord helps those who help themselves.

I got serious about all this in 1972 when I transferred to the University of Washington and began my junior year with classes in novel writing and short story writing. Many books, articles, columns, poems and plays later, I can tell you the Muses have yet to show up when I'm working. And, I can tell you, that writing spark is still there.

What you've done the last two days, and what you're going to be doing over many coming days, is become a better writer by writing. Over time, it will be easier for you to say what you want to say in the way you want to say it. I could tell you writing will become easier but it would probably be more honest to say writing won't be as hard.

It's seldom if ever easy. It can, if you work at it, get less hard.

Part of the myth of the Muses is the misguided belief, the sad hope, that at some moment, in a frenzy, you'll easily dash off of a complete novel. Yes, *O Father* was written in a three-day frenzy but it wasn't easily dashed off. It was a lot of work concentrated into a lot of hours over only a few days.

There's a flip side to this. If you wrote your novel in a Muse-induced state, if a goddess merely channeled herself through you, it wouldn't really be *your* novel, would it? But, nine weeks from today, it will be *your* novel. Your *completed* novel. (Eight weeks and four days!)

5
WEEK ONE, DAY 4

LWS: "Fun" and "Satisfying" Aren't Synonymous

It's Day 4 of the first week and, just as you suspected, writing is not fun. Yes, it's a delight to think about, to imagine, to daydream of being a novelist. ("Successful novelist," needless to say.)

But, as you may have discovered in the past when you started penning your opus, and as you can confirm after three days of writing this week, actually writing your novel is not fun. Neither is writing a play. A poem. A work of nonfiction. And so on.

Small wonder I bite my thumb at those in any profession who tell the public, "Well, if it weren't fun anymore I just wouldn't do it." This from adults. Adults! People old enough to know better who tell that falsehood about their being a captain of industry, a professional ball player, a wealthy and aged entertainer who could easily retire and still live like royalty. But you get the idea.

Perhaps they aren't lying to us. Perhaps they're simply being imprecise. What they may actually mean is "if it is no longer personally satisfying anymore." But that's a different kettle of fish, isn't it?

If you began this project believing "I am going to have a hi-ho time doing this!" I must hasten to inform you—to bring sad tidings of no joy—that writing a novel is a hi-ho time except for almost all of the actual writing. And that's why so many would-be novelists never become novelists. That's why you may have a partial manuscript (or two or three) tucked away in a desk drawer or saved on an ancient computer hard drive. That's all right. We all do.

An advantage of having a timeline (only nine miserable weeks!) and a daily word count (only so many hundred stinking, rotten words today!) is they help you arrive at the satisfying part of this. Fortunately, that can be a daily occurrence. Small satisfaction couples with small satisfaction and, over time, comes the larger joy of having completed an entire novel. A whole book. Beginning. Middle. And end.

Yes, some eight and half weeks from now you may look back and declare, "That *was* fun!" And you'll believe it. Until you start your next novel.

6
WEEK ONE, DAY 5

BD: The Advantages of Writing What You Know

If you're writing an entire novel over a three-day weekend, or over nine weeks, you don't have a lot of time for research. On the other hand, you don't want to be inaccurate. Or at least not flagrantly inaccurate.

When I was cranking out *O Father* like so many pounds of sausage ... . Let me rephrase. As I quickly wrote *O Father*, I used my own town for the setting. Store here, church there, neighboring suburb like this or that. And I made the main character (protagonist, for you English majors) a dad in his late thirties because I was a dad in my late thirties. He went to Mass at a local Catholic church one evening because—on that evening of writing—I went to Mass at my parish. (Was that a time of prayer or of taking more notes for the next day's writing? Yes. And yes.)

You know a lot. And, it could be, a lot of it you don't know that you know. Some of what you know is technical or specialized. If you're a lawyer or a welder. If you grew up on a farm or in the city. If you went to all all-girls school or dropped out at sixteen. And on and on.

O Father opened with a stakeout because, a few years earlier, I had driven around part of Seattle with my then eight-year-old daughter to see if I could spot the mammoth station wagon that had ploughed into our car a few months earlier—a hit and run—when my wife and I had been driving in that area. Later, out hunting, I didn't spot the culprit's vehicle and I don't know what I thought I was going to do if I had. In any case, I knew it was a stupid idea to have my daughter with me but ... there we were. And there, years later, was the opening scene to my novel.

That gave some truth to the scene but, being fiction, it was filled with baloney, too. With lies. Good novelists are good liars.

So, today and for the rest of this undertaking, if you need a setting, character, emotion, and so on, consider what you already know. Yes, by all means, change it, tweak it, blur it a bit so you don't get sued. So you can mumble, "Any similarity between the characters and real persons is purely coincidental."

Or impurely.

If that horrible high school teacher absent-mindedly picked his nose, make it a she who uses her pinkie or a paper clip to remove ear wax. The reader's revulsion will be the same.

7
WEEK ONE, DAY 6

LWS: Never Throw Anything Away

It's quite possible that over the past five days you've written some words, phrases, paragraphs or whole pages that, on reflection, you find are far less than what you had hoped they would be.

Or, in the vernacular, "God, that sucks!"

Let's assume God is already aware of the fact.

As your days and weeks of writing go by, you'll continue to come up with what appear to be clunkers, both large and small. Do *not* delete them, erase them, tear them into a thousand pieces, or burn them like a High Lord Censor at a medieval piazza bonfire.

Save them because ... you never know.

It could be that as you reviewed your day's word count you were tuckered out and everything in this whole, disgusting world seemed to stink. Including a hefty chunk of your day's writing. Sometimes it's hard to accurately or fairly judge your writing when you're too close to what you've just written. You think it's the bee's knees. And it ain't. You think it ... reeks ... but, after resting and further review, you see it ain't that bad. In fact, parts are pretty durned good. Pretty durned good, indeed.

If you had immediately destroyed it, it would be gone. And, trust me on this, when you thought back on it you would realize some of it *was* good and since you no longer have it, it will seem even better as time goes by. What was that phrase you used? What was that snippet of dialogue?

Poof.

Like Hamlet's papa, that ghost will haunt you for a long, long time.

If you keep it, at the very least, you can confirm "This really does stinkeroo" and get on with your life, haunt-free.

Then, too, that bit of writing may fit in well somewhere else. Just right. Or what seemed to be a character way out of place may be the star of a future book. That scene that wandered off on the wrong track and went on too long may be the beginning of Novel Number Two.

For example: "By the pricking of my thumbs, our man, Romeo. Here he comes!"

Awfully glad I saved that one. Awfully.

Now go finish today's word count, back up and print today's work, and take pleasure in adding it to your growing stack of material. Then enjoy your day off tomorrow. Return on Week Two, Day 1 ready to complete 400 words. You can do it.

8
WEEK TWO, DAY 1

BD: Writers Are Jotters

Let me begin by confessing that I don't want to begin. Not today. I wrote some of this book yesterday and I don't want to today. But, to complete a book one must ... .Yes. Continue writing it.

You've had a day off, haven't you? Hope you enjoyed it and that you're rested up and reasonably ready to go today. Four hundred words, right? Right!

In our last exciting episode, Willie mentioned not throwing away any writing no matter how useless, or terrible, it might seem. Today's topic is similar: Jot down any passing idea about your novel no matter how useless, or terrible, it might seem.

It doesn't matter *how* you take notes as you're writing your book but it does matter a lot that you *do* take notes. One reason is, once again, if you don't write it down and later can't recall exactly what it was, you'll be certain it was one of the most brilliant flashes of insight you've ever had. And you'll be certain you'll never have it again.

On the other hand, if you record it somewhere and look at it later you may decide:

1. This is just god-awful.
2. This is brilliant.
3. This is somewhere between 1 and 2.

I strongly advocate scratch paper. You may do better sending yourself an email, text, or voice mail. I (almost always) have a bit of scratch paper and pen in my shirt pocket. You may not have a shirt pocket. You don't have to do this the way that I do this or the way that any other writer does this but you would be wise to do it in *some* way.

Once you start entering into the world of your novel, a stray thought about the setting, a few lines of dialogue, a piece of a character's back story or some other flotsam may wash up on shore. Grab it before the tide sweeps it away.

In my own experience, I tend to find those "objects on the beach" when I'm out walking, when I'm swimming laps, when I'm at Mass, or when I first wake up in the morning. I was amused many years ago when the local newspaper's police report said a woman had phoned the cops to say a suspicious looking man seemed to be writing down car license plates. The police noted that she had no idea what he (what I, I assume) was jotting down.

I try not to think about my writing as I swim because idea can pile up on idea and with no shirt, no pocket, no pen or scratch paper, I have to remember them on my own.

When the ideas start to flow at Mass, I try to discreetly take out my paper and pen so I don't disturb those around me. I'm not sure I'm successful.

My pajamas tops do have a pocket but rolling over onto a ball point pen seems like a bad idea so instead I use the dash-to-my-pen-and-paper method if something pops into my head. Yes, having pad and pencil near the bed would be a good idea. I doubt I'll do that. I haven't so far. Slow learner.

You may have noticed that, for me, the ideas, the

connections, the sweet tidbits come when my mind is somewhere other than I Have to Write This Stupid Book, whichever stupid book I'm working on. (On which I'm working, for you English majors.) I suspect the same will be true for you.

And, of course, make your notes long enough and legible enough so that you'll know what the heck you were thinking. ("BFL L FF." Was that the "big, fat lady loves french fries" or the "barfly left finger frints"? "Frints"? Was that last letter supposed to be a P?)

What to do with all those notes? Put them in one spot, whether a folder or computer document. Check back on your "Novel Notes" from time to time and you may discover just what your book needs for that day's writing or how to get your plot out of a dilemma that you've fallen into. (Yes, yes, "into which you've ... ")

9
WEEK TWO, DAY 2

LWS: When and Where You Write Best

It probably doesn't help you much if I say the best place to write is England, unless you're in England or can easily get there. Probably worse if I say the best time to write is the late-sixteenth and early-seventeenth century, unless you have a time machine.

It's true that going on a "writer's retreat" is lovely and having a (paid!) sabbatical can be a delight, but at that retreat spot or on that leave, each day you need a place to write and a time to write. You need those day after day after day because a book becomes a book by a writer working on it day after day after day.

Let's talk about time first. It doesn't matter if you're a night owl or an early bird. There's probably a best time of the day for you when it comes to writing. Some writers discover, much to their horror, that they may be night owls but they do their best writing first thing in the (early!) morning. That means while they're working on a book they have to get to bed earlier than they like to in order to get up earlier than they ever wanted to.

Or it might be because of other demands—family, job, life—some writers can't get to their manuscripts until late in the evening. That's when the household is finally quiet and they can have that forty-five minutes or an hour to themselves. As you're discovering, if you didn't already know, having a block of quiet and uninterrupted time makes a huge difference in your ability to concentrate and write.

True story: When my own family was pestering me in so many ways and I had very little time to myself to work, I'd crack off a sonnet. There! At least I got something done! ("When, in disgrace with fortune and men's eyes/I all alone beweep my outcast state"... in the loo. Really. "Papa! Papa! I have to ..." "Give me a minute, Hamnet!" Yes, the little dear's name was "Hamnet.")

Find *your* time. Find *your* place. And keep them sacred. If only for another seven weeks and four days, when your novel will be completed.

10
WEEK TWO, DAY 3

BD: When a Character Refuses to Obey You

This may not have happened to you yet but I wanted to put it near the beginning of this book so that you'll recognize it when it does happen. If it happens. Don't be frightened but there may come a time when one of your characters—even a reliable one, one you really like—will say or do something on his or her own. It's ... *aliiiiiive!*

I'll give an example. In my novel *Pope Bob*, two recovering alcoholic priests are talking about how their drinking influenced their lives and their ministry. The older of the two, the one who's helping the younger, says:

> "During that particular blackout, I missed my mother's rosary on Tuesday night and funeral on Wednesday morning. I was to be the celebrant. I was going to say the Mass. One of my sisters never forgave me and I never held that against her. She was right. Three years later she was killed in an automobile accident and hadn't set

foot in a church since Mom's funeral. Wanted nothing to do with a religion that had a priest like me. And still I drank."

I, the author and creator of that character, was astounded! I had, and have, no idea where that came from. Yes, it came from me but what he shared was so sad! There's been nothing in my life like that. Nothing I recall reading about that's similar to it.

But there it was.

In some ways, writing a novel is nothing more, and nothing less, than putting some people into a situation and watching them try to get out of it. And eavesdropping on them as they do it.

Over the next seven weeks, some of your characters may surprise you. (No, don't poke them with a stick to make them say or do something startling.)

Then, too, in your early chapters you may be giving yourself a vital piece of information, the value of which you're completely unaware of until you reach a later chapter. Or even the last chapter. This—like the runaway character—can happen even if you're following a strict outline.

Say, for instance, a character needs a job and, what the heck, you put her in a supermarket. Checkout clerk. Fine and dandy. Doesn't matter. Minimum wage. Then, many weeks, and many chapters, from now, *say!*, she could have stashed a body in the walk-in freezer in the back of the store, if she's the culprit. Or she could find a body back there and figure out who-done-it, if she the heroine.

Whatever you have planned in your outline may pale in comparison to what develops from the story itself. (She wanted to keep the body close to her. What a ghoul! Or … she was the only one observant enough to see what was behind those pallets of rocky road ice cream and smart enough to know who could have left it there. What a girl!

(Or woman, depending on how old you make her.)

In the meantime, write your 400 words for today and then enjoy the glorious feeling of "I'm done with that!"

11
WEEK TWO, DAY 4

LWS: Symbolism, Maybe

Well, here you are starting the second half of the second week! Today's topic: To symbolize or not to symbolize, that is the question.

As you well know, all novels are filled with symbolism and if yours doesn't have any by now then ... . Not so! Pulling your leg. You can write an entire novel with no symbolism if you don't like symbolism and you don't want symbolism. What do I mean by "symbolism"? I mean something that stands for, or represents, something bigger. That item has "symbolic meaning."

Never mind what some professor said to you at university about "all truly great writers fluf-fluf fluf-fluf, so on and so forth." Certainly, you had to agree with him or her in that classroom and when you took your exams or wrote your papers but ... .

What a load a fecal material.

You can't be a true lady without wearing a corset. You can't be a true gentleman without waxing your mustache.

You can't be a true novelist without cramming your book with symbols.

"Ah, look how the author uses water!"

"Ooh, see how the author puts a mirror here and there and here again."

If you like symbols, use them. If you don't, don't.

If you took any literature courses in high school or college, quite probably the books chosen by the schools or teachers were ones with a lot of symbolism because:

A. The teachers liked symbolism, a lot.

B. The teachers studied those same books and that same symbolism when they were students under teachers who liked symbolism, a lot.

C. Talking about symbolism in a book is a jolly way to spend (to fill) a class hour.

Let me be clear: I, personally, have nothing against symbolism. Take it or leave it. Which I did. Used it when I wanted, didn't use it when I didn't want it. I advise you do the same. I'd lay a wager, and give you very good odds, that if in the future one of your novels becomes a book used in classrooms, some teachers and students will find symbolism in it whether it's there or not.

Let them. Perhaps, like the runaway character Bill spoke of yesterday, you put it in there without being aware of it. But remember symbolism doesn't make a novel great. What makes a novel great is that it tells a great story.

Now go to work on yours.

12
WEEK TWO, DAY 5

BD: Tone and Voice

One big reason there's an annual Hemingway write-alike contest is that Hemingway wrote like Hemingway. He didn't start out that way. If he submitted some of his very early attempts as contest entries, the judges would say, "Not even close! Well, okay, a little close but not close enough."

Hemingway became Hemingway by writing. Ditto with Chaucer, Emily Bronte, Dr. Seuss and every other writer who has a "voice." Whose writing has a certain "tone." Yours may already have that. And it may not. The only way I know to develop that voice and tone is to write, write, write. You can read a lot of writers, you can read a lot of books about writing, but ... there's no substitute.

Over time, your own style will emerge. Choices of words. Sentence structure. Punctuation. Yes, all within the rules—more or less—but with your particular spin. (In other areas, it's what makes "your" golf swing your golf swing or "your" home-baked chocolate chip cookies your home-baked chocolate chip cookies.)

The good news in today's message is you don't have to do anything to develop your voice (or strengthen your voice) except write and that's what you're already doing. Yes, writing is always hard but, I suspect, by the time you finish the novel that you're writing now, it will be a little easier because it will be easier for you to use *your* voice to say what you want to say in the way that you want to say it.

Easier more often. Not always. Never always.

In the first twenty years of my full-time freelancing, I had about two dozen books published. Some fiction, some non-fiction. Some for kids, some for adults. Some serious, some humorous. Some prose, some poetry. And the occasional play. (Apparently, I have trouble focusing, eh?) By then my voice was my voice. In a serious book, there likely was some humor. In a humor book, there were a few serious points.

This may sound like bragging and that's not my goal here. (I take great pride in my humility.) I like my writing voice but it wouldn't have happened without those very early books. The ones I did long before I had anything published.

Not to discourage you, but I wrote ten books before I had one published. You probably won't need that many. I know that if I had quit after number nine, I wouldn't have published any. And to encourage you: One of those first ten was later published and sold well.

Consciously ("Ooh, I like the way that sentence sounds.") and subconsciously ("I wrote that? Huh. That's good."), you're developing your voice and like that golf swing or those cookies, it's a lovely thing to have.

13
WEEK TWO, DAY 6

LWS: You Are What You Read ... Sort Of

There are forty-seven distinct genres within the "novel" category ...

All right, I just made that up. Certainly, someone somewhere came up with such a list (*cough*-dissertation-*cough*) but it's not of much use here. That's a polite way of saying it doesn't matter, unless your novel is somehow about all the distinct genres within the "novel" category.

When you were younger and your mother let you use the "good"—meaning sharp—pair of scissors she always warned you "Don't cut yourself!" Today's advice is almost that obvious.

Just as it's easier to write what you know, it's easier to write what you read. Mystery. Fantasy. Historical. Young adult. Middle-grade. It makes no difference what you like. (Some people like tea more than mead. Imagine!) If you love science fiction and you've read tons of it, it will be easiest for you to write science fiction.

Probably.

You know the ins and outs of that sub-genre. You know the unwritten rules and the unspoken laws. Say, for example, you're writing a murder mystery and you don't introduce the killer or offer any clues pointing to the killer until the final chapter. Bad form that.

At the same time, it's hard not to compare your current work to some of your favorite writers who have been penning their wonderful novels for years and years. Be of good cheer: they didn't start out as great writers. They got to the point at which you met them by doing what you've been doing over the past two weeks and what you will continue to do over the next seven weeks.

Furthermore, pennies to pounds they look at their self-imposed daily writing assignment and react just as you do with yours: *Ugh!* See that? You're already developing a professional attitude. And, like them, you're climbing over that "Ugh!" and completing that assignment.

Odds are your writing will sound a bit like theirs and that's all right. Part of learning to write a novel is imitating novelists you like. The ones who have influenced you. After all, if you think what they did was good and you want to be good, why wouldn't you emulate their style? As Bill mentioned yesterday, over time—as you churn out thousands and thousands of words—their style will fade and your style will emerge. You may always write *like* so-and-so but your voice will be distinctly present. And obvious.

Finishing Week Two, aren't you? By the end of today's writing, you'll have more than 4,000 words on paper. Well done! Enjoy your day off tomorrow and return on Week Three, Day 1, ready to complete 500 words per day. You can do it!

14
WEEK THREE, DAY 1

BD: The Three P's of Writing

Years ago I interviewed a woman who had the same publisher I did for my humor books. I was visiting with her for a newspaper article I was writing and she was explaining the three P's of professional writing.

1. Perseverance.
2. Prayer.
3. Postage.

She hadn't had any easy life. Her husband was killed in a bicycle accident—a head injury in pre-helmet days—and it was up to her to raise their young children. She had a great sense of humor and began writing jokes for Phyllis Diller and Joan Rivers and then began some public speaking. She mentioned that her first speech had been scheduled for November 23, 1963: the day after President Kennedy was killed. That gathering was cancelled.

But she stuck with it and, over time, had some books published. She reached that goal, she told me, because of the three P's. A writer has to:

—Keep writing until the book is done! (Persevere!)

—Keep praying (if he or she is the praying kind) or, at the very least, maintain a positive attitude.

—Keep putting his or her material "out there"—getting it to publishers or posting it online or self-publishing it.

Yes, when she and I began our careers, getting material to a publisher or agent involved using postage. (I've been at this a long time. Back to the age of manual typewriters, when dinosaurs roamed the earth.)

By now you may be far enough into your manuscript that you suspect, or are convinced, it was a bad idea to try to write a book and writing *this* particular book was an even worse idea.

Don't give up. Not yet. I'm usually a little farther along in a manuscript before I decide the book I'm working on was a stupid idea and that I'm doing a horrible job writing it. The first few times that happened I was startled. Then I came to expect it and recognize it when those doubts popped up. The concern can be even greater, the stakes higher, when one has a contract to write that book and one has already spent the advance. (Been there/done that.)

When that happened to me, I had the luxury of putting the manuscript aside for a week or so and then rereading it from the beginning. I always discovered (was relieved to discover) it wasn't as bad as I had feared and some of it was rather good.

I could set the manuscript aside for a week because I was sure I could finish a book. I had completed a lot of them. You don't have the luxury of taking a few days off because a large part of the challenge you've stepped forward to meet is completing a book following a strict schedule. (You can take a wee break, if you need it, as you write your next novel.)

Just write today's word count, today. And tomorrow's tomorrow. It may be what seems likes a mess is really a wonderful plot turn or character development that will *really* make your story. You'd never know that, discover that, if

you hadn't just kept going.
So keep going.

15
WEEK THREE, DAY 2

LWS: How to Show, Not Tell
Part I: Narrative

Like "write what you know," the advice to "show, don't tell" falls under the vast heading of "Things About Writing I Have Been Told a Thousand Times."

(Say, that's in the passive voice, isn't it? Most often, active voice has more punch. Better clean that up and make that vast heading "Things Jerks Keep Telling Me About Writing.")

Yes, you've heard this, read this, thought this many times. That's because the basics of good writing are, well, the basics of good writing.

Let's say, for instance, a plot involves a woman who has encouraged her husband to kill a higher-up and the author notes: "She was filled with remorse." (Or, active voice, "remorse filled her.") That's "telling." "Showing" might be for her to sleepwalk and "see" the blood of the poor dead fellow on her hands and mumble "Out, damned spot! out, I say!"

Forgive me for digressing, but I have to confess I've always wanted to see a line of Lady Macbeth hand creams and body lotions. Get rid of wrinkles, age spots, and so on. And I nearly gave that character a first name but "Betsy Macbeth" was my favorite and it sounded too much like a farm-fresh adolescent who won the blue ribbon in pie-making at the county fair.

We'll talk about naming characters another day but to return to ... uh ... don't tell me.

Yes! Quite right. *Don't* tell me. *Do* show me.

How do you show something to your readers? Since your novel is narrative, dialogue, and description, I'm going to say ... narrative, dialogue, and description.

I'll talk about narrative. Tomorrow Bill will write about dialogue. (That doesn't sound right. I should *write* about narrative and Bill should *talk* about dialogue.) Then I'll ... describe ... how *to show* using description.

But, you may argue, isn't narrative telling? It is. So how does a writer tell the reader something without telling the reader something? Good point! The answer is a line or two of narrative can do more than tell what it's telling, at first glance.

If you had a character who was a mean and nasty man you could write, "He was a mean and nasty man." That's telling. Pure and simple and awful. Instead, you could say:

—"While no neighbors had actually seen him kick a puppy it would have surprised none of them to learn that he did. Regularly."

—"It wasn't that he thought himself better than others. Totally self-absorbed, he remained unaware there were others."

—"The only time the corners of his mouth turned up in what might be mistaken for a thin smile was when he made one of his young, female employees burst into tears."

How you talk about that meanness depends on the type of novel you're writing and the tone you're using. If a serious one for adults, it might be his ex-wife has a restraining order against him. If a lighthearted middle-grade novel, perhaps even the school bully crosses the street rather than walk directly in front of his house.

The same can be done for setting. ("The old woman's house wasn't too hot ... if you were accustomed to visiting saunas." "The town's south side would have been best known for the stench of the meat packing plant if the high crime rate didn't always take top billing.")

A similar way to do this, but one that can easily be overused, is to drop in a simile or a metaphor. The simile uses "as," like" or "than" to compare two things: "He was as greasy as a pound of cheap bacon." A metaphor makes an analogy between two things or ideas. "Even her brief glance was a laser beam that forced him to stare at the floor."

No, wait. "Stare down at the tips of his shoes."

You don't have to know the names of these figures of speech to use them well. It can help to run through a list from time to time to see if there are some you might like to sprinkle in here or there.

16
WEEK THREE, DAY 3

BD: How to Show, Not Tell
Part II: Dialogue

I've always loved writing dialogue for two reasons. It was easier for me than narrative and, in the days when my self-imposed daily quota was page count I could whip through several pages using very few words:

"Huh?" he asked.

"You heard me," she answered.

"You can't be serious!"

"Don't tell *me* what I can or can't be!"

And on and on. Five pages done and I was free for the rest of the day.

For me, it was even better than most want-to-be novelists' favorite (worthless) self-imposed daily-quota gauge: time. "Oh, yeah! I'm going to be at my desk for one full hour." Up for coffee. Answer phone. Stare out window. Make paper-clip chain necklace. And on and on and on. Wow, writing is *hard*. A full hour and only twenty-three words.

And this was before computers and the Internet. Back in the day when it took some effort to be distracted and not actually do any writing.

And now back to today's topic.

You can show the readers some things about your characters by what they say and how they say it. A pompous ass (is there any other kind?) may use big words or toss in foreign phrases that the others don't understand. Why? Because, the reader knows, it's a lovely and nasty way to make those others feel inferior. Then, too, the reactions of those other characters will show the reader something about them, too.

They could: Nod, pretending they understand and hoping the fellow doesn't call their bluff. Roll their eyes, signifying they know this guy is a jerk. Ask what that word means, demonstrating they're eager to learn and won't be intimidated.

Or ... .

Mr. P. Ass could use a big word or foreign phrase incorrectly. And, again, others' reactions would tell the reader something about them.

Some of this is obvious. It's offered here just as a reminder. An educated person would sound educated. A kid would sound like a kid. But a fellow who has gone to the big city and made a success of himself may slip back into the local lingo (P. Ass choice for "local lingo" being "regional patois") when he gets flustered or returns home for a visit.

(I'm reminded of a woman I know who lives in the Northwest and was heading back home to visit her mom in Virginia for a week. "When I get back here," she said, "I'll reacquire my southern accent for a while. The longer I'm there, the stronger it gets.")

A character's idioms, exclamations, and language "tics" can reinforce who he or she is. "It's fourth and long." "Saints preserve us!" "So I was, like, 'What?', and she was, like, 'Duh!'"

41

Two more examples: The presumably uneducated and dim-witted character who occasionally lets a college-level vocabulary word slip in there: "I'm sorry I'm late. We were inundated at work." Or, the other side of this coin, the character others assume is educated and bright who sometimes flubs basic rules of grammar: "Just between you and I, I think this is amazing."

As you get farther into your novel, as you get to know your characters better, let them speak for themselves. Write down what they say. You may be pleasantly surprised.

And more than a little freaked out that such a thing can happen.

It can.

17
WEEK THREE, DAY 4

LWS: How to Show, Not Tell
Part III: Description

I don't want to complain but I really think I should have had the day that dealt with dialogue. I *am* a playwright, after all.

Description can be challenging for any writer. It's been said if you can describe a table in the middle of a room, you can write just about anything. Describe it in a way that keeps the reader's interest, that is.

There's the rub. (Nice phrase that. I had meant that sentence to break poor Hamlet's tension. If you could look closely at the original manuscript you would see it says: "There's the rum!" The good prince—ho, ho, ho and a bottle of ... well, you know—was going to have a nip or two as he continued to mull things over. Misread. Misquoted. Such is life.)

But back to that table. How can a table *show* the reader something? Maybe it doesn't have much of anything to show. It's simply part of the furniture. Wooden and rickety in a poor person's home. Chrome and steel in a dynamic businessman's office. Small and handmade in a monk's cell.

It's not as if you have to go on page after page describing a table. You can if you like. You have God-given free will. And if you like novelists that do go on page after page with their descriptions and you want to write as they write, then by all means go on and on.

However, just because you *can* do something as a writer doesn't mean you *should* do something as a writer. Or at least, not do it all the time. Yes, if it's the equivalent of *Citizen Kane's* sled, Rosebud, then spend some paragraphs on it. But if it's just ... a table ... and the reader only needs to know the room has a table then keep the story moving right along.

Even in a brief description—perhaps especially in a brief description—it helps to keep in mind that adjectives and adverbs are the equivalent of punches. (No, we are not talking about rum again. We are referring to fisticuffs.) They have an effect but never the power of a good kick. A leg is more powerful than an arm. If you want to describe something, to show the reader something, use a leg, use a verb, to do it. *Smacko!*

"In the center of the room *was* an old, wooden table with a broken leg."

"In the center of the room a wooden table *teetered* on three full legs that *reached* the floor and one that *leaned* on a fat phone book as if it had been *broken off* at the ankle."

"Was" vs. "teetered," "reached, "leaned on," and "broken off."

Again, you would be ill-advised to overuse that type of describing but used judiciously, it can please the writer and the reader.

Most simply put:

1. Don't rely on forms of the verb "to be." Consider stronger verbs.

2. Don't go thesaurus-crazy, coming up with all sorts of

action verbs all the time. (Even the Rockettes don't fill a routine with nothing but high kicks.)

18
WEEK THREE, DAY 5

BD: Coming Up with Names for Characters and Places

I tend to have a lot characters with Irish surnames. I suppose it's because I have a lot of relatives with Irish surnames and, because I'm an Irish-American Catholic, those are the ones that pop into my head.

Surname means last name. I learned that my first day of student teaching. My teacher had a list of rules and one was I was to use only her surname. I didn't know what that meant so I didn't address her by any name until I could get my hands on a dictionary. (I was a terrible teacher and never went beyond my student teaching and a little substituting.)

I do try to come up with other names that are pretty clearly other nationalities or ethnic groups. Polish names, French names, Italian names. Russian names, Filipino names, Japanese names. It's not foolproof but it does help me have characters beyond my own little Catholic ghetto. (Unless, of course, I want a story that focuses on a Catholic ghetto.)

A main character in *O Father* is named Bob Johnson. He's a Tulalip Indian. (That's a tribe a little bit north of where I live in western Washington state.) And the main character in *Pope Bob* is named Bob Johnson. He's an Irish-American Catholic from Omaha because I am both of those, too. (Write what you know, right?)

When I wrote *Pope Bob* I chose "Bob Johnson" because I knew two Bob Johnsons in my own life and I knew it was a pretty common name. My main character needed a common name. It was only years later, when I was rereading *O Father*, that I remembered I had a Bob Johnson there, too. Later still, rereading *The Hidden Fortune,* I spotted yet another one. (This time a minor character.) I couldn't change the name in *O Father* or *The Hidden Fortune*. They had been published long ago. Even so, I wanted that common name in *Pope Bob* so ...

Being the author, I said, "This is how I'm going to do it." And I did.

Now you, being the author, can name your characters any name you like but keep in mind that some names are associated with certain preconceptions or stereotypes that could get in the way. You would have a tough time with a family named Hitler or Stalin unless, as part of the plot, they were related to *the* Hitler or *the* Stalin. If you named your hero Richard M. Dixon readers would have a tough time not thinking Richard M. Nixon.

It could be you want that name association. Maybe it's something she, your character, has to live with. (During the Bill Clinton administration my wife Monica and I had to live with being another couple named "Bill and Monica." Fortunately, that all died down.)

You can name characters after someone you know. (It's safer if that someone is dead because dead people are less likely to sue.) You can give a tip-of-the-hat to old classmates or cousins or ancestors by giving minor characters their names. (I've done that.)

You can make up names that amuse you or that sound sinister or innocent or ... . But you get the idea.

And you can do the same for places. You're not locked in to places (cities, states, countries) that are real. Yes, use a real locale if you like. No, don't bother if you don't like. One of the joys of novel writing is that it's *creative* writing. And you are the creator.

19
WEEK THREE, DAY 6

LWS: How to Choose Just the Right Word

As if writing isn't hard enough, you not only have to come up with 500 words per day but they have to be 500 of the *right* words. On the other hand, you don't have to use iambic pentameter like I did, do you? No, you do not.

In fact, you don't even have to know what iambic pentameter is. (It's a style of rhythm or beat or meter. Not "one-two-cha-cha-cha" but "one-TWO, one-TWO, one-TWO, one-TWO, one-TWO." Ya-*hoo,* ya-*hoo,* ya-*hoo.*)

So what's a "right" word and what's a "wrong" word? All words are right, and all words are wrong, depending on where and how you use them. Let's take the name "Bill" for example.

"Bill went to the store and Bill bought a half gallon of ice cream and Bill didn't share any of it with Little Willie."

And compare:

"Bill went to the store and he bought a half gallon of ice cream and the self-centered pig didn't share any of it with Little Willie."

It's not hard to see that "Bill" and "he" and "self-centered pig" all refer to the same person.

In the same way "he bought a half gallon of ice cream and the self-centered pig didn't share any of the ice cream with Little Willie" wouldn't be so great either. "Ice cream" and "ice cream."

Unless, of course, you wanted to repeat for effect. (You can *repeat* it for effect, you can *repeat* it for style, you can *repeat* it for emphasis.) And you can do that without setting the readers teeth on edge, as long as you don't do it too frequently. In fact, some words are so unique, it's better to use them only once in your entire book. Really. A word or words such as *ubiquitous, penultimate, slovenly* or *poo-poo head.*

The same with some phrases or idioms unless—again—it's for effect.

"'It's hotter than the lids of hell,' said the captain." And then, two pages later, as part of a narrative. "The day dawned warm and was certain to be hotter than the lids of hell."

You could, however, have one of the lieutenants note, "Today is going to be hotter than the lids of hell" if you wanted him to be a toady or a suck-up to the captain. (Know your audience.) Then you're not *saying* he's a sycophant, you're *showing* it.

You probably know a lot of this. Or all of it. And more. No offense intended. Just little reminders. As you finish week three, I hope you're not getting bogged down in all the piffle and prunes Bill and I are slinging at you.

Just keep telling a good story. That's all. A good novelist tells a good story.

Now get busy with today's assignment and enjoy your break tomorrow.

20
WEEK FOUR, DAY 1

BD: Going with Your Strengths and Overcoming Your Weaknesses

Welcome back! By now—three long weeks!—you've probably discovered some parts of what you've been writing have come more easily than other parts. Maybe it's description. Or narrative. Or dialogue. Maybe it's giving some of the back story on a character or following the basic outline you came up with before you began on Week One, Day 1.

For me, it's always been dialogue and, for a time, I was a little concerned that my fiction had too much of it. Even though I was setting a daily word-count as my goal, I was still coming up with pages and pages that were mostly characters talking to each other.

It took a while for me to develop a way to toss in the "he said" or "she added" without messing up the flow of the conversation but still letting the reader easily know who it was that was saying what.

Even back in school, dialogue was always easiest for me and what I enjoyed the most. Or, it was what I enjoyed the most because it was easiest for me. It's probably no surprise that my favorite novelists are also strong ... dialogue-ists? Dialogue-ers? Dialogue-writers.

It can be tempting to think that whatever you're best at, your strength, "doesn't count" because it's not the comparative torture that some other parts of writing can be. Or because you know there are world-class writers who are tremendous at another aspect of novel writing that you're less than sterling at.

After writing for many, many years, I've decided it's not unusual that a writer tends to dismiss his or her strengths and assumes the really great writers are those who are more capable in another area. In a similar way, under the general heading of "entertainer," the actor admires the singer and the singer wishes he or she could dance and the dancer secretly longs to also be a comedian and the comedian hopes to break into acting.

Even after having lots and lots of books published, I still sometimes think my non-fiction work isn't *really* a book or my novel isn't *really* a book because ... .

Other works of non-fiction are so much more scholarly. Or novels have long, complicated plots. I suspect most of my non-fiction could easily be read by a sixth-grader. And most of my novels are linear: this happens, then this happens and then this happens. (Maybe a few flashbacks, but not many.)

On the other hand, it's been nice having readers say, "I like your writing because it's easy to read." That's a very pleasing review, unless you're writing only for yourself or you don't want, you know, *ordinary* people to read it and enjoy it.

So go with your strengths. And hang in there with your weaknesses. You'll get better in those areas, too. And they don't have to be perfect. They don't have to be outstanding.

Few writers can do it all. And none do it all—all the time—in every book.

21
WEEK FOUR, DAY 2

LWS: The Myth of the Suffering Writer

Reviewing what the two of us have already written, I think Bill and I have tended to focus on how hard writing can be. (Abandon hope all ye who enter here!) But what if you aren't having a horrible time writing? What if this isn't as hard as you thought it was going to be? What if you aren't suffering for your art?

Well, then you're doing it wrong!

Just kidding. If things are going well, then stick with it, eh? If it works, don't go mucking it up.

The idea that a writer, or anyone, has to suffer to *really* produce is a cartload of hokum. It's a romantic myth. That's not to say some writers haven't had incredibly hard lives and they've used that experience, those experiences, to pen some touching and insightful works. (Writers write what they know, right?)

On the other hand, some accountants have had tough lives and they, too, may be better at their vocation because of it. (More diligently making sure another family doesn't squander its money and end up in the poor house, for example.) And so, too, with some teachers, some rabbis, some members of just about any profession or vocation you can think of.

You can be a tremendous novelist even if you're happily married, have great kids, and enjoy your day job. Even if you only drink socially (or not at all), have never inhaled, and shun caffeine and tobacco.

In the same way, you can write a great book without having that "cabin by the lake"—your holy of holies, your retreat, your sanctuary—in which to write it. That's good news, isn't it? I assume you're not at that lake right now. Not looking out the huge picture window to gaze on a vast expanse of lake and forest and ... . No! Wait. French doors. Looking out those French doors, which are open just a few inches so you can feel the breeze, take in the pine-scented fresh air, listen to the ...

Blah, blah, blah. If you *did* own that "perfect" cabin, you'd have to worry about taxes and insurance and a leaky roof and ... . Does that cabin have indoor plumbing? No? Then you might end up doing some suffering there on a cold, dark night when nature calls and you have to head for the outhouse.

22
WEEK FOUR, DAY 3

BD: How Much Research Is Too Much Research?

It would probably surprise you to learn that some novelists, whose plots span not just generations but eons, are their own "research department." They want their books to begin at the beginning. If not the beginning of time, then perhaps the beginning of the shaping of the continents or the foundation of a culture that's thousands and thousands of years old.

One would hope they like researching.

On the other hand, there are some novelists who know they have to get some facts right (Boston is in the east, Los Angeles is in the west) but don't much care about the minor stuff. And, since it's their book, they get to decide what's minor.

They don't need to know the latest slang being used by teenagers even if they have a teen using slang. They don't need to know what bookstore is next to what peep-show place in a seedy part of a city even though they're going to have a scene or two in that part of town.

Fiction is fiction. And your readers, God bless them, will accept the world that you create and the rules you create to govern that world. In each genre, in every genre, they will accept your book as a member of that genre as long as you follow the basic guidelines for that type of novel.

You know that. You know what kind of novel you like to read and you know what can and can't happen in it. If, as an author, you follow the guidelines, you'll be fine. And doing a little creative writing within the guidelines is just fine, too.

I'll give you an example. Much of my book *Pope Bob* takes place in downtown Seattle. From the time I began writing it until the time it was published, a lot of that part of the city had changed. That was okay. I can say the library is here and the Catholic cathedral is there, and they still are. But this particular tavern or restaurant on this particular corner may now be a upscale coffee shop or gravel parking lot. This street, which was two-way, may now be only one-way. And on and on.

I feel safe saying if you try to be as accurate as possible in all details you will:

—never get your manuscript completed;

—make a mistake that a sharp-eyed reader will take delight in pointing out to you; or

—be dismayed to discover that—as the world and all that's in it keeps changing—whatever was correct when you wrote the manuscript has now become incorrect.

When I began *Pope Bob* telephone booths were common. By the time I had it (finally!) ready for publication, cell phones had all but eliminated them.

Again, some details matter: Don't confuse President Washington with President Lincoln. Don't put Des Moines in Ohio or Boise in Iowa. Don't have New Orleans on Eastern Time or let water come to a boil at 200 degrees Fahrenheit.

And other details don't matter if you don't want them to. Who cares if, really, it was sunny or rainy in New York City on July 4, 1998? If you find out it had been sunny that day and your plot needs it rainy, let it rain! But! There are some dates and places you can't mess around with: readers would have a hard time believing your New Yorker spent an uneventful day in Manhattan on September 11, 2001.

As you write your manuscript, don't get sidetracked with details. If you want to go back and check something, jot down a quick note to yourself but *keep writing to make that day's word count.* (You can also put that note in your manuscript at that spot: [Hey, your name here, what's the deal with this?] Put it in a nice red font, too.)

When I began writing fiction, it was harder to check facts. One needed a book or a library or another reliable source. A book might have been on hand when the question came up but the other ways of research usually required going somewhere or talking to someone. (More on interviewing later.) These days a novelist can be zipping right along on a daily word count, have a questions, tap a few different keys on the old keyboard, and be bombarded with information. And a host of lovely distractions.

Don't confuse writing with researching. Your writing may need some researching but not while you're writing your daily word count.

23
WEEK FOUR, DAY 4

LWS: Why Writers Write

Why are you writing a novel? (No, not "attempting to write a novel." You are *writing a novel!*)

Certainly, it must be for:

a. money
b. fame
c. power
d. all of the above

Or none of the above. Any or all of the above might be nice but the likelihood of that happening is not tremendously in your favor. It happens for some. And happens to a certain degree for others.

If you want to get rich, choose a profession that pays very well or marry someone who's loaded.

If you want to be famous, become skilled at a world-class level in some area or post a ludicrous and/or embarrassing video on the Internet.

If you want power, get elected to national office or be the funding source for those who are elected to national office.

If you want to be a writer ... write.

And why write? Because you want to write. Because, on some level, you *need* to write. When you don't write, when you haven't written for a while, you feel uneasy. You know that, again on one level or another, you *should* be writing.

The cliché is if you can quit writing, you're not a writer. As with many simplistic statements, that's true and not true. Maybe you'll be able to quit after this novel. You have one novel in you and, having completed it, you're perfectly content to never write another.

Not everyone who climbs a mountain wants to climb another and another and another. He or she just wanted to climb that one particular mountain. That one right there. And every time he or she sees it, or thinks about that experience, there's joy.

That might be you. This is your one novel. This is your one mountain. There's absolutely nothing wrong with that. Good for you for making the trek you're on now.

24
WEEK FOUR, DAY 5

BD: Should You Let Others Read Your In-Progress Manuscript?

You're starting to really get a stack of manuscript pages now. And, even if you haven't told family, friends, and coworkers what you've been up to, they know you've been up to something.

How do they know? You go off and do something by yourself six days a week. You tend to be more distracted even when you're around them. And you pull out scratch paper and make cryptic little notes. (Or have been texting yourself.)

They may not recognize the telltale signs of the novelist at work but those *are* some of the telltale signs of a novelist at work.

You are a novelist at work on *your* novel.

So should you show them, or him or her, what it is you're doing. Should you, at this point, share your work with someone else?

That depends on you. And that's why the correct answer could be yes or no or—*shrug*—it doesn't matter. As you read on, you'll probably be able to detect the answer for me is no, no, no. I don't let anyone see my manuscript until I'm done with my manuscript. But then, I have a very large ego and I've never been a fan of writers' groups.

When I took writing classes back in college, students regularly shared their work with other students and, of course, with the teacher. I liked it when someone made a positive comment about something I had written. A good sentence. A believable scene. Humorous dialogue. (Looking back through my rose-colored trifocals, *gee!*, I can't remember anyone ever saying anything negative.)

And it was helpful to read a professor's comment or critique of something I'd handed in, and to meet with him or her one-on-one and go into more detail of what worked and what needed work.

That was in a relatively controlled environment, of course. The professor could keep students from savaging a peer and from just saying nice things for the sake of being nice.

I don't think your family, friends, or coworkers would tear your incomplete manuscript to shreds but I think they're likely to say "That's nice! That's really good!" The problem is you don't know if they're just saying that or if they really mean it. (Yes, they might add, "And I *really* mean it!" but still ... .) Would they say "I don't like it" if they didn't like it? That doesn't seem likely.

It could be they really can't judge if it's good or not. And, you suspect, even if they think it's horrible, they're going to say it's great.

Or they might focus on some small element or detail that doesn't matter in the big picture and an even lukewarm comment on it could have you focusing way too much attention there when you would be better off moving forward day by day. It could have you doing too much editing and rewriting when you should be writing! There will be plenty of time for editing and rewriting after you have an entire manuscript to edit and do some rewriting on. (Only a light edit, certainly. A little rewriting.)

Maybe a very good friend whose judgment you trust or your sweetie-pie could do a good job reviewing your partial manuscript. Odds are either of them knows how to tell you a truth that hurts without being hurtful and when either says he or she likes something you know it's not a little white lie.

A writers' group might be able to do that, too. That would probably work better if you already belonged to the group before you began this challenge. Then you would know how they critique and how they offer constructive suggestions that really are constructive.

At some point you're probably going to have to let someone else read what you wrote. For me, usually it was my wife, Monica, who read the first, completed draft. (So sad to say, she died of uterine cancer in 2013.) She was good at catching typos and mistakes and—over her decades of doing that—had developed two code phrases for "What the heck were you trying to do in this part!" One was: "I stumbled a bit here." The other: "I think I know what you're trying to say." Either meant my writing wasn't clear or I got too wordy or too cute or too ... any other number of ways of messing up a sentence, a paragraph, a scene, a chapter.

(She was so very kind. A year after she passed away I wrote the novel *Mildred Nudge: A Widower's Tale*. And later, a non-fiction book, *On Your Pilgrimage Called Grief: A Guide for Widows and Widowers*, on making it through early widowhood. Write what you know even if it's something you never wanted to learn. Or maybe especially if it's something you never wanted to learn.)

I suggest that unless you know it helps you to have someone read your work-in-progress, wait until after the full nine weeks, and the full manuscript, before you have someone else look at it. And, even then, put it away for a while and reread it yourself first before letting someone else read it. We'll have more on "put it away for a while" ... in a while.

25
WEEK FOUR, DAY 6

LWS: Knowing the Rules and Knowing When to Break Them

Today's message is simple: You need to know the rules for proper writing. Grammar, punctuation, and spelling. (Although, to you in the States, I hope you realise that when you spell "realise" as "realize" you are incorrect. Not that you are labouring in vane but it is the King's language that you colonist-rebels have bastardized. Or would that be bastardised?)

As you write for these nine weeks, don't let grammar, punctuation, or spelling slow you down. You can't imagine the many faux pas I made (to borrow a phrase from our French brethren) when I was moving full-tilt toward the opening of a new play. The play's the thing!

The novel's the thing!

If you are going to break a rule of grammar or punctuation or misspell a word—and you can choose to do so—it is best if you know you are breaking that rule or misspelling that word. And it is best if you are doing so for a specific purpose.

It may be to show us something about a character. It may be for comic relief. It may be because English is a living language and that particular rule is all but dead and has been ignored by many writers for many years. Or perhaps the traditionally preferred spelling really isn't the preferred spelling anymore.

This isn't to say you need to know all the rules that fill a fat grammar book. But, once your manuscript is completed, you need to have someone who does know them (or knows most of them) read what you have written. In the publishing world, this would be an editor or a copy editor.

Copy editing isn't writing. And, truth be told, copy editing is easier than writing.

Most if not all aspects of getting a book published are easier than the actual writing of the book.

In general, if you aren't sure about the rule or the spelling, and you want to follow the rule or spell the word correctly, look it up.

But not while you are doing your day's writing. That always comes first. You can do that research later that day. Or another day. Or after you've completed the entire manuscript. Just make a note to yourself to find the answer later.

Now on to your last day of writing for week four. And then a day of rest!

26
WEEK FIVE, DAY 1

BD: Interviewing Others ... and Yourself

Last week we wrote about the Goldilocks aspect of research: How much is too much, how much is too little, and how much is just right for you.

Today's topic looks at how to find and interview someone you think will be helpful for you to present a believable (and interesting!) portrayal of whatever or whoever it is you want to portray.

Again, I'll use my book *Pope Bob* as an example. A lot of that takes place on Seattle's Skid Road and when I was a newspaper reporter I did a few feature articles on some of the people who were a part of that scene. (Some homeless, some who worked in overnight shelters, some who were prostitutes, some who were ordained and whose ministry was to street people, and more.)

I knew something about alcoholism because ... well ... . Let's just say I quit drinking a long, long time ago. (Thanks be to God.) But I didn't know about chronic alcoholism and so I chatted with a classmate who had spent many years working for the county as a counselor to that population. (For a time, he drove the "detox wagon" that would pick up folks who had passed out on the street.) And I visited with the father of one of my daughter's classmates who was director of a drop-in center in that part of the city.

Two points:

1. If you stop to think about it, you probably know some things that you don't realize you know. Or, more accurately, you don't appreciate that you know those things because you think everyone knows them. That everyone has experienced what you have.

When I was teaching a class on writing at a rec center a student lamented that he had never done anything exciting and so he had nothing to write about. I asked him his profession and when he told me, I said: "Have you ever gone into a burning building and helped someone get out of it?" "Oh, sure," he answered, "but everyone I work with has done that." He had spent more than twenty years as a firefighter but had "never done anything exciting or interesting." Compared to his fellow firefighters.

2. Most people like talking about themselves and about what they do if the person asking them about it is respectful and truly interested. You may know someone (the old classmate, the parent of the kid on your kid's soccer team, the retired woman across the street, and on and on) who knows a lot about what you want to know something about. And what that person can tell you will add some lovely color and realism to your story.

Ah, but you might be shy. How to ask? What to say? Have your questions ready and simply tell the truth. You're working on a novel and ... . And, I bet, they'll be happy to help and, far from snickering at the thought of you (*you!*) writing a novel, they'll think that's wonderful. (And they may mention they've been wanting to do that, too, at which point you can tell them there's a moron author who says a person can write a novel in nine weeks and he's written a book about that.)

27
WEEK FIVE, DAY 2

LWS: Moving the Story Forward

By the time someone says "to make a long story short," it's tempting to note, "Well, it's too bloody late for that, isn't it?"

Your novel isn't a long short story. It's not a simple little piece that could be covered in a few hundred words if you hadn't been stuffing it with fluff and nonsense like it was some poor goose getting force-fed to be nice and fat for Christmas dinner.

I take that back. You can stuff anything you like into your novel because it is your novel. But, methinks, you would be better off (and any reader would thank you) if you stick with the story and keep the story moving right along.

Yes, it's tempting to slide in an essay on whatever it is you would like to write an essay on. And, yes, you can have your main character or some other poor sap begin with "Well, here's what I think about ... ." Immigration or salaries or the poor or the rich or white sugar or vegetarians or running barefoot or any number of peoples, conditions, causes, historical inaccuracies or ... .

A novel is not a book of essays. Not a book of poetry. Not a play. Not anything but a novel. And a novel tells a story.

I know it's tempting—with that miserable daily word count—to fill a daily void with words that count toward a total for the day but don't really count when it comes to telling your story.

And, I believe, you have a good story to tell. It's one you've been thinking about telling for some time. One you want to tell. One you want to tell *well*.

Well ... that's why once you've set the scene, or once the characters have said what's needed to be said during a conversation, once the lovely little plot elements have been dropped into the places in which they needed to be dropped, move on!

28
WEEK FIVE, DAY 3

BD: Write in the Middle

When you finish today's writing—and I have every confidence that you will!—you'll be halfway through your novel.

Wow!

Four and a half weeks done and four and a half to go. (Yes, mathematicians, it's not halfway by word count. Your word count after today will be 11,700 of 25,200 total.)

Remember back in the old days, six or seven weeks ago, when you were just thinking about writing your novel and maybe talking about it with other people, and now ... .

You've come a long way, you novelist you!

I have a suggestion for later today but feel free to ignore it.

What's that you say? You've been ignoring a lot of the suggestions in *this* book and have simply been writing *your* book? Well! All I have to say to that is this: Good for you for writing your book!

When you're done with today's word count you may

want to spend a little time rereading what you've written during the past four and a half weeks. There might be some item you wanted to include in the last half of the book but have forgotten about. A thread you can pick up; a person or detail that's slipped your mind.

You might be pleasantly surprised to discover there are some passages that you really like! (I think this will happen.)

You might be relieved to see some sections you weren't so sure about really do work just fine.

You might see a section or two you would like to rewrite. (Not now! Not during these nine weeks. Make a note about it but don't get bogged down with rewriting and editing until you're done writing.) Don't panic or obsess or shake your head in discouragement. It could be what seems like a mistake now will turn out to be just the lovely twist you need for the plot or a character in the second half of your novel. Be at peace. All will be well.

And if you do that first-half review you will certainly see that a daily word count mounts up into a sizable manuscript-in-progress if you stick to that word count over a period of time.

And you have!

29
WEEK FIVE, DAY 4

LWS: Momentum Is Your Friend

As Bill said yesterday, "Well done!" You have completed no small number of words and today you're back at it. It's the wise writer who uses momentum to keep surging forward and that's exactly what you have now.

Think about it: You have your routine. You're accustomed to the (bloody, stinking) word count due each day. And you've alienated your friends and family who have learned to leave you alone when you're writing. (That or you've grown accustomed to getting up in the wee hours of the morning or staying up in the late hours of the night to reach that (bloody, stinking) word count due each day.)

You may have never written this much on a previous attempt. You may have reached what you thought was the midway point on another manuscript and then, for any number of reasons, abandoned it.

This time it's different. This time you not only can succeed (complete the manuscript!) but you will succeed (complete the manuscript!) because you not only know how to succeed but have been using a method that works.

You don't have to do anything new or different to finish your novel.

You can just do what you have been doing.

Bit of a relief that, eh?

So go write 500 words today.

30
WEEK FIVE, DAY 5

BD: Booze and Drugs

Let's start today with booze. No, not start the day with a belt or two but start today's message with a little bit about drinking and writing. Or using drugs and writing. (Beyond the occasional aspirin or antacid tablet. Beyond a prescription that keeps you healthy in body and mind.)

You probably know biographies of some famous writers who were also famous boozers or drug abusers. And so, one might conclude, alcohol and drugs don't interfere with one's writing but one would be wrong.

I have no doubt that those famous writers either wrote when they weren't zonked out of their heads or they wrote at a period in their lives when they weren't abusing alcohol or drugs. Or if they did manage to get some words down when they were in their cups and such, those words were not as good as they would have been had they not been buzzed, tipsy, or completely blotto.

This isn't a temperance lecture or a "just say no" pitch. (There aren't any bumper stickers that read "Don't Drink and Write.") It's making the point that a human mind works better without chemical interference and where that chemical starts to interfere varies from person to person.

If, for example, someone in your writers' group typically has two glasses of wine at dinner and then sits down at the keyboard and creates wonderful passages in her novel, you may think if you had a glass or two, your writing would automatically improve.

Nope.

But, you may be objecting, doesn't that also mean some writers can sniff this, smoke that, or shoot up the other and be great writers because the amount they use doesn't chemically interfere with how their minds works?

To which I reply: You cannot do your best work, no matter what your field may be, if you are abusing alcohol or drugs. And if you want to argue that, you are perhaps arguing about your own use of either or both.

And I add: *In vino veritas* (in wine, truth) means you're likely to spill the beans about something a friend told you in confidence, not that you reach *Truth* at the same point where you start slurring words and wobbling a little when you get up from a chair.

31
WEEK FIVE, DAY 6

LWS: Why Multifaceted Characters Are Always in Character Except When They're Not

One of the joys of writing fiction is playing God. What a treat to create people and places and situations and jumble them all together and decree, "Well now, let's see you get out of *that!*"

Except, of course, when you play God as a writer there are still some guidelines if not rules. You can do whatever you want but if you do some things, your reader will decide:

—Well, that's an incredibly stupid story. Or ...

—That character is totally unbelievable.

Since you want neither of those to happen (assuming you want neither of those to happen unless you *are* trying to create an incredibly stupid story or a totally unbelievable character) then you must pay attention to those guidelines. (Yes, even as a little-g (lowercase g) god, you *must.*)

Needless to say, what you want to do is write a wonderful story with great characters. And perhaps what you need to hear said is: *You can do that!*

Today, a bit on characters, a simple guideline. If, at this point in your novel, you're concerned with some of your characters (a little flat, a little dull, a little boring), it can help to remember no one is perfect. Yes, this applies to you (and to Bill, of course; and—to a limited degree—to me) but here I mean you don't want any character to be perfect. And you don't want any character to be perfectly imperfect.

The very proper matron sometimes lets a blue expletive escape from her pursed lips. The psycho-killer pets puppies or always sends his mentally slow cousin flowers on her birthday. Everyone now and again makes a mistake. Everyone now and again gets something right. Everyone now and again does something out of character and that's what helps make that character believable. And much more interesting.

And we're at the end of another week, aren't we? Five hundred words today and a day off tomorrow!

32
WEEK 6, DAY 1

BD: Overusing Favorites

As you can continue to develop your style, or as you continue to find or define your voice, you may fall into a trap that a lot of writers fall into. (Including yours truly.) It's not fatal and can be corrected after you finish your manuscript. (Only twenty-four days to go! You started with fifty-four.)

The trap is overusing certain punctuation or styles. For example, one would say Bill Dodds frequently relies on:

—parentheses (Really? Ya think?)

—em dashes (Yes, but—in his defense—they can be so lovely.)

—ellipses (That may be so or ... it could be he's ... perfected ... their use. Not likely.)

Then, too, Bill seems to lean toward short, incomplete sentences and short paragraphs.

Guilty!

Guilty as charged!

This kind of overuse is something to be aware of in your

writing but there is no "right" amount. That combination—heavy on this, light on that—is a large part of what makes your voice your voice in the same way that certain ingredients and the amount of each make your recipe your recipe.

If you're preparing lasagna for family and friends, how much garlic is too much garlic? And how little is too little? The right amount is the amount you like and the amount the ones who will be eating it like.

There *can be* too much. And sometimes the way you find that out is they gasp or cough or tear up or simply ask "How many pounds of that stuff did you put in here!"

Just as some recipes use the disclaimer "salt to taste," my advice is "use your favorite punctuation and style to the degree that you like, but if your readers have a hard time with it and you want to keep those readers, cut back."

You don't want that garlic—those parentheses, em dashes, ellipses—to dominate, to overwhelm, your lovely dish, your lively novel.

33
WEEK 6, DAY 2

LWS: Your Novel in Three Acts

While it's true that my plays had five acts, most plays in your time have only three. Or two. Or one. Why mention that when you're not writing a play? Because a play, a screenplay, or a novel each has a particular structure and—surprise!—often it's the same one.

In your time.

In *my* time novels didn't exist but my point is a structure that works can make for a novel that works better. Certainly, you can use a novel approach to your novel but if, at this point in your writing, you're beginning to think "Zounds! How am I going to bring this all together? When do I begin to introduce this or change that?"

A basic formula can help. It's one used by many, many writers and it's worth considering.

> Fillet of a fenny snake,
> In the caldron boil and bake;
> Eye of newt, and toe of frog,

> Wool of bat, and tongue of dog,
> Adder's fork, and blind-worm's sting,
> Lizard's leg, and howlet's wing,
> For a charm of powerful trouble,
> Like a hell-broth boil and bubble.
> *Serve over rice or mashed potatoes.*

Excuse me. Wrong notes.

The formula is: at one-quarter, end act one and begin act two; at three-quarters, end act two and begin act three

This is much easier, given the scarcity of howlet's wing (not to mention particular howlets are now on endangered species' lists) and the cost of fillet of fenny snake. (Cheaper to buy a complete fenny snake and fillet it yourself, but what a mess, what a bother!)

At each turning point, something shifts in the plot or in a character. In a novel of 160 pages, those points would be around page 40 and page 120. (Or, in word count, at 25 percent and 75 percent.) In a 100-minute movie, they would be around 25 minutes into the film and at about 75 minutes. You can check this for yourself. Pick a film, make those divisions, and see what happens near those points.

That being said, there are many ways to structure a novel (a play, a poem, an essay, a grocery list) and if this tried-and-true three-act method works for you, lovely. If not, the Novel Constabulary will not come knocking at your door demanding a rewrite or threatening to haul you off to gaol. Excuse me once again. To jail.

34
WEEK 6, DAY 3

BD: History and Classics

Today and for the next nine days we will examine the history of the modern novel, tracing its roots back to the time of ... .

Just kidding.

You don't need to know the history of the novel to write a novel. And you don't have to have read classic novels to write a novel. If you know the history, great. If you want to learn the history, fine. If you've read a lot of classic novels, great. If you want to reread them, fine. Probably, neither the history nor the reading can hurt and either might help.

What you need to do to write a novel is write a novel. And you're doing that.

I say this as someone who has written many novels but doesn't know the history and hasn't read a classic since he was forced to in college. It's not that I'm anti-academic. I'm saying it's not necessary unless you want to include something about the history of the novel in your novel or you want to employ some devices that have been used in early novels. It's not necessary unless you're writing a novel in the same genre as a classic and want to use a similar style. Or try them out in a different genre. Be oh-so avant-garde.

Likewise, you don't need to read any classic hard-boiled detective novels unless you're writing a hard-boiled detective story and want to stay true to the form. (Or if you're writing one that's soft-boiled, like *O Father*.)

I'd mention some classic science fiction and romance novels but I don't know the titles of any. I've never read any. And I've never wanted to write any.

(And now you, in the middle of writing your science fiction or romance novel, think, "Ah ha! That explains a *lot* about this Bill Dodds.)

Today's point is this: There are many of people who will tell you "You cannot write a novel until you _____." Fill in the blank.

At times, you may have told yourself that. "Until I learn this or read that. Until I retire or I get that new computer. Until I _____." Fill in the blank.

Baloney.

At this point in our relationship, you may have deduced "Any moron can write a book."

This moron says that's absolutely true.

Not to imply one has to *be* a moron, but that hasn't stopped me. If anything, just the opposite. I was too stupid to realize I was too stupid to write a book. And so I did.

35
WEEK 6, DAY 4

LWS: A Wee Tip on Threes

Just a wee tip today so you can get right to your writing. When it comes to threes:

1. Make them consistent or inconsistent.
2. Put the punch at the end.

All right and off you go!

No? Hmmm. Then consider this:

1. When you have a series of three, make them all the same (consistent) or none the same (inconsistent).

For example: "We were eating our lunch, having a good time, and thinking about our future." (Consistent.) "We were eating our lunch, it was a lovely time, and thoughts of the future filled our heads." (Inconsistent.) We were eating our lunch, having a lovely time, and we thought about the future. (Mixed.)

Generally speaking, readers don't like mixed even though they may not be aware a series is mixed. "One for the money, two for the show, three to get ready and go on four." Eek! If you're leading with numbers, keep leading with numbers. If you're using a noun, keep using a noun. Or keep using a verb, adverb, adjective, and so on.

But, of course, if you want to give the reader a bit of a shake, mix it up but be aware that you are mixing it up and don't simply be messing it up.

And 2. When you have that series put the biggest, worst, best, smallest, at the end. The superlative goes last. Small, smaller, smallest or big, bigger, biggest, depending on which makes more sense.

"The reviewers crucified, criticized and critiqued the author." Since crucified is far more serious than critiqued, it should go last.

"The reviewers whined about the plot, the size of the paragraphs, and the font style." Since the point is the reviewers were being overly picky, the smallest (stupidest) complaint would be the last one in the series. (As if you, the novelist, chose the font! Really!)

Now off you go, ready to plot, to write, and finish today's assignment.

(Wrong, right? A series: "*to* plot, *to* write, and *to* finish.")

36
WEEK SIX, DAY 5

BD: How to Write Faster

I was impressed with Little Willie's being so brief yesterday so I'll try to be the same today. One thing many years of writing have taught me is that sometimes I can't come up with the word I want when I want it even though I know there's a right word, the *perfect* word. Then, too, sometimes there is a fact or bit of grammar that I'm unsure of (of which I'm unsure) but that's no reason to stop.

Or even slow down.

When I hit that spot I type in "xyz" and move on. After I've reached my word count for the day I can go back and check for any "xyz" inserts and, often, by then the word will pop into my head. Or, in the case of a fact or bit of grammar, I can look it up and fix it.

Again, this is *after* I've reached my daily word count.

37

WEEK SIX, DAY 6

LWS: The Trouble with Numbers

Is Bill implying he can be briefer than I can? Not bloomin'
likely.

Pay close attention when you use numbers because, if
you're like many writers, your verbal skills are far greater
than your numerical skills.

Check your math. Take a second look at all figures.

I'm not (usually) one to tell tales out of school but I
know for a fact Bill submitted a non-fiction manuscript with
an introduction that included "Here are twenty-five chapters
that examine ... " (or some such) when the book had only
twenty-four. It is true I scribbled "The Sixth Part of King
Henry III" (when I meant "The Third Part of King Henry
VI") but I corrected that myself.

Enjoy your day off, after today's work.

38
WEEK SEVEN, DAY 1

BD: Three Small Mistakes

Well, well, well. Look who's completed two-thirds of a novel!

As I mentioned in an earlier chapter, this is the point at which I'm sure my idea was a bad one and my execution of it was even worse. This how-to book is no exception. Here I am thinking just that.

But it gives me great joy to think there you are with two-thirds of your novel completed. I know it could be you've never written this much of a book. And so, from now on, each day spent on this one is a record-setting personal best!

And there are only eighteen days to go.

As much as I would like to take all the credit for your success to this point (and beyond), I suppose a portion of it goes to you. Some 99.999 percent.

Now, on to three small mistakes and how to avoid them:

1. Singular and plural with he/she/they. Make sure singular and plural agree. Sometimes this means doing a little editing to avoid an awkward sentence. ("Look who's completed two-thirds on their novel." No. "Look who's completed two-thirds of his or her novel." Correct but clumsy. "Look who's completed two-thirds of a novel." Brilliant! I wish I had written that. Oh, wait ...)

Let's pause here to point out another living-language situation. Just as "he" referring to all people singular gave way to "he or she," so now singular he or she is giving way to "they." "The witness said the driver wore a hat but they had no coat."

2. Introductory clauses and phrases. They need to agree with the subjects they modify. ("Climbing the stairs to my bedroom, the lightning flashed and thunder rumbled." They climbed the stairs? You meant you did, right? "As I climbed the stairs to my bedroom, the lightning flashed and thunder rumbled.")

3. Overuse of ordinary words. Placing the same ordinary word too close to itself can cause a reader to stumble (and an editor to wince) unless it's done on purpose for effect. ("When they finally arrived dinner began. We could finally eat." Not good. But this would be okay: "When they— finally— arrived, we could—finally—eat." Or: When they finally arrived dinner began and, at last, we could eat.")

39
WEEK SEVEN, DAY 2

LWS: The Perils of Perfectionism

Fortunately for you and me and all writers, we live in an imperfect world and there's no such thing as a piece of perfect writing. (Although, at times, a bit of writing can be almost a piece of perfect tripe or an editor can seem to be a perfect jerk.)

Now that your manuscript has some size it may be tempting to think "I should start going back over this and making it better."

Not yet. There will be time for self-editing later and when that day comes don't confuse "I can make that different" with "I can make that better."

There's always tinkering that can be done but there must come a point where, in the words of Pontius Pilate, *"Quod scripsi, scripsi."* What I have written, I have written. (I advise this as someone who spent a week obsessing "Romeo and Juliet. No! Juliet and Romeo. No! Romeo ... .")

Any (honest) professional writer will tell you that once a piece reaches a professional level any over-tinkering only causes damage. And, once a piece is published, the writer always sees things he or she wishes could be changed, adjusted, edited, nudged, nuanced, or axed. In part, that's why quite a few professionals don't read their own work once it's published.

Your novel will not be perfect.

Your novel may be very, very good.

You novel, even if it is not very, very good, is still a novel you have written and that is a tremendous accomplishment.

Don't let its being imperfect stop you from completing it or from taking pride in that accomplishment

40
WEEK SEVEN, DAY THREE

BD: Dealing with Naysayers

We begin today's lesson by pointing out that sometimes it's the horse's ass that says, "Nay!"

And, as you know, we all run into that type of person much too frequently. Sometimes they're unavoidable.

Little by little, day by day, you've been writing your novel. And little by little, day by day, they can take potshots at what you're doing and at you for trying to do it.

But, of course, you're not just *trying* to do it. You *are* doing it.

No wonder they find you and this project so irritating. Who can blame them? Odds are they've thought about writing a book and they may have even begun one. Or two. Or five. Odds are they quickly abandoned the plan because (who would have guessed it?) writing a book is hard work. Lonely work. Work that is far, far, far from glamorous.

You're like the friend or coworker who "turned against" his or her smoking or drinking or out-of-shape peers by quitting smoking or stopping drinking or getting in shape.

You, dear novelist, are *really* annoying! That's true even if you haven't slipped into the nasty habit of pointing out, "If I can do it anyone can." Yes, this is true. But, no, those other people don't want to hear it.

The truth is that even some established novelists get a strong negative reaction from others. "His book isn't so hot. Anybody could have done it." Maybe so, maybe so. But the "anybody" making that crack didn't and the one who wrote the book did.

Ignore the horse's ... . Ignore the naysayers. Listen to the folks who love you and are so pleased that you're doing something you've wanted to do for so long.

41
WEEK SEVEN, DAY 4

LWS: Choosing Words Wisely

I wish to set the record straight.

It's true that I'm a genius sock puppet and playwright but that isn't why my plays are filled with words that seem so intimidating today. I used the vocabulary of the time and that body of words—spelling, pronunciation, definition—changes over time. I'd have gotten nowhere if members of the audience looked at each other and asked, "Just what the deuce is that supposed to mean?" (Instead of giving a mate an elbow in the ribs, snickering a bit, and pointing out, "Well, that can be taken two ways, can't it?")

Writing a piece to demonstrate your knowledge of a huge and impressive vocabulary is easy. You simply pen: "These are big words that I know." And then go on to list them.

If, however, your goal is to tell a story well, then you would be smart—and wise—to avoid letting that huge and impressive vocabulary get in the way of telling the story in a way that your readers can understand it. So that they can even enjoy it without tripping over those impressive words.

I'm not saying to dumb down your work.

I *am* saying don't choose a word in some sad attempt to prove how bright you are.

And, naturally, keep your reader in mind. If your piece is for children in middle school don't use all the more advanced vocabulary words that you might use for a novel directed at adults. This seems obvious, doesn't it?

So then:

Eschew obfuscatory verbiage!

42
WEEK SEVEN, DAY 5

BD: Enjoying the Journey

As I mentioned (LWS: twice!) before, it's when I'm about two-thirds of the way through a manuscript that I start to bog down. It isn't just the doubts, it's the lack of newness to the whole project. New can be terrifying but it's also exciting.

It's also usually at about this point in my own writing that I begin to think about what I'd like to write next. (Yes, *that's* the book I really want to do. It will be *so* much better than this not-quite-done one. It seems so much more interesting.) I may even start to make some notes on the next one and hope I can finish the current one as quickly as possible.

But, of course, when I reach the same point in the new one, I'm likely to find myself in the same position as I am with this one. A bit bored with the present and very much looking forward to the future.

And that's a shame.

I'm reminded of a underclassman I knew in high school.

I went to a seminary—a boarding school—and it was a *big* deal to get to leave the grounds on Tuesday or Thursday afternoon and walk to a 7-Eleven store that was about a half mile away. After living on institutional food for a long time, we considered a Slurpee a real treat. I remember this one fellow who, in the middle of slurping his drink on Tuesday stopped to say—with great feeling—"I can hardly wait to come here on Thursday and get one!"

I hope this hasn't happened to you. (With your novel, not your soft drinks.) I hope it never does. But if it has, if it does, I suggest that you make those notes for the next book and then put them aside and enjoy what you're writing right now.

43
WEEK SEVEN, DAY 6

LWS: God from a Machine (*Deus ex Machina*)

Now that you've added some lovely layers to your characters (none is completely good or bad) and an amazing number of twists and turns to your plot (ha! reader didn't see *that* one coming), you may find yourself rapidly approaching a place in your manuscript where you have no way to resolve the conflict.

You do have some sort of conflict, right?

It can be tempting to:

1. Leave it all ambiguous and claim it's up to the reader to figure out what happened. (Please imagine that, on hearing such a suggestion, I am making a rude sound by sticking out my tongue a bit and blowing air from my mouth. What, in your time, became known as a Bronx cheer or the old raspberry.)

2. Introduce a new character, ability, or object that solves all the problems. In my time, and in some plays, it was a god descending from heaven. An actor being lowered on to the stage by a machine. Rope and pulley and box and such. This

deus ex contraption might have flown, so to speak, half a millennium ago but ... please. Nowadays? Not quite. (And now kindly imagine my giving a hearty guffaw if you have had an inkling toward using this to complete your book.)

Oh dear, oh dear. What can you do? Take a long walk or a hot bath. Take a hot bath after a long walk and let your creative mind simmer. I'd wager the solution is right there and you just don't see it yet. You may not see it until you write it. Have faith in the story you've written up to this point, have faith in the foundation you've laid and the characters you've created.

They will solve the problem.

You simply write down what they do.

(And, of course, take tomorrow off. Only two weeks to go!)

44
WEEK EIGHT, DAY 1

BD: Endings That Surprise the Writer

I don't want to alarm you but at the end of next week your novel will be finished. Yes, that's good news but it can also be disturbing news.

Only twelve days to complete ... everything?

Assuming you followed Little Willie's advice and took that walk/soaked in that tub, you can see the ending from here. Or at least what you think the ending will be. Keep pushing toward it even if you aren't convinced it's the ending you want.

If you think it is the ending you want, you may be surprised to discover it isn't the ending to your book once you get to the point of actually writing the ending to your book.

Let me make a confession. You might have gotten the idea that I always crank out novels in a matter of months (if not days). You probably got it because I probably mislead you. *Pope Bob* took more than fifteen years but not because I worked on it for fifteen years. I worked on it, put it away, forgot about it, remembered and felt bad about it, did a little more on it, put it away ... and so on.

By the time I finally got around to finishing it I thought I had finally figured out what the ending would be. I was wrong. About the ending. It was only when I got right up to it, when I was going to be writing it in the next couple of days, that I realized it wasn't *this,* it was *that.* Of course it was that!

Over the next twelve days, keep moving toward your ending. You're so very, very close to finishing your novel and it may hold a surprise for you. If it doesn't, don't be disappointed. That probably just means you're better than many of us at outline, plot, character, conflict, and all the rest.

That's a definite possibility, you know. You may have a lot more talent than a lot of published novelists. You certainly have more basic talent than some!

45
WEEK EIGHT, DAY 2

LWS: Keeping Pace

It's hard not to run to the end when the end is in sight. To rush through the last scenes, to condense or combine them, to skip them completely and—*voilà*—your book is finished.

Or …

To increase the daily word count to get done faster.

But …

There's no need to get there faster.

It's been slow and steady to this point. (That and, at times, bumpy.)

That has worked. Stick with it.

(What? You think today's lesson is too short? Why? You're doing what you should be doing. Or you will be doing what you should be doing once you quit reading what I've written and get on to what you need to write. For today.)

46
WEEK EIGHT, DAY 3

BD: Evaluating How-tos on Writing a Book

It's hardly news to you that there are a lot of books, magazines, websites, podcasts, blogs, videos, and heaven only knows what else on how to write a book.

I didn't wait almost two months into this project to first mention that because I figure after almost two months you can't return this how-to book and get a refund. Not *just* because of that.

After working on your novel for more than seven weeks you not only have a lovely stack on manuscript pages and the proven ability to work on a book day after day, you also have a much more discerning eye when it comes to all those how-tos.

Now it will be very clear to you that:

—Some have a few suggestions that are helpful for you.

—Some offer you nothing new.

—Some have cockamamie theories that make no sense in the world of reality. (Your world.)

—Some promote ideas that are more likely to hobble

you than help you.

After your seven-plus weeks of novel writing you have a much better idea of what works for you and what doesn't. What helps you and what doesn't. The only way you could have learned that was by doing exactly what you've done since Week One, Day 1.

Surprise! Consider this an out-of-the-blue bonus. You've earned it.

47
WEEK EIGHT, DAY 4

LWS: The Advantages of Writing a Series

Ye gods, only nine days left in this nine-week adventure and there you sit with so much to say and only four thousand five hundred words with which to say it. Small wonder you may be tempted to cram in as much information as possible. Now that you really know some of the characters there's so much more that you'd like to share with readers. (So much more those characters would like to share.)

Consider a series. It worked well for me and for many writers since my time. Probably one of your favorite authors has penned—I really do use that verb too often—a series and you looked forward to the next installment. (Some novelists have turned a few main characters into a major industry: a money-making machine.)

The advantage of a series is you already have a head start on your next book. Those lovely little bits and pieces you can't use this time, those delicious paragraphs and plot twists you sliced from this manuscript because they just don't fit, can be the seeds that take root, grow, and blossom in volume two.

Even if you don't have too much to say between now and the end of next week, it may come to be that after you've completed this novel you'll realize you'd like to visit these people and those locations once again. To share (and to discover for yourself) just what these characters have been up to.

48
WEEK EIGHT, DAY 5

BD: A Writer's Ego

Seven and a half short (or not so short) weeks ago you may have thought:

—"Aw shucks, I can't write a novel. Who am I to even *think* such a thing?"

Or:

—"I've read some incredibly poorly written novels of late. I *know* I can do better than *that*. A monkey with a laptop could do better than that!"

Or:

—A combination of both. Wildly vacillating between "I can't, I can't, I can't" and "Anyone can, anyone can, anyone can."

Well, you were wrong.

You can. (You're almost done, for heaven's sake.) And not just anyone can. Some people, including a goodly number who love to read novels, can't write a novel. And of those who can, not many attempt it. And of those who attempt it, not many stick with it. You can write one and you're going to complete one.

That's not to say your work is better than what's out there but, it seems safe to speculate, it tops any monkey with a laptop.

A novelist needs a healthy ego. It takes some sense of self-worth to decide not only "I can write this" but also "and others will want to read it." That gets easier over time, after others have read some of what you've written and—they honestly tell you—they like what you've done.

A healthy ego can also accept helpful criticism and suggestions, and reject any comments that don't help. (Or are just plain wrong.) The ego separates the wheat from the chaff.

And a healthy ego keeps the writer in check, reminding him or her "you ain't all that, but you are *something!*"

49
WEEK EIGHT, DAY 6

LWS: Epilogues

Still concerned about finishing all this by the end of next week? No, not the word count. You're humming right along on that! No, I mean a concern about tying up any loose ends. As a novel reader, you hate lose ends. You know how disappointing—if not truly frustrating—they can be. Now as a novel writer, you don't want to disappoint or frustrate your readers.

To avoid that, it's helpful to read through your manuscript at a brisk pace not with an eye toward editing but to see if any unfinished business pops up. A wonderful and effective way to tie up those loose ends is with an epilogue.

I, personally, loved them. (Using a closing monologue (epilogue-style) in a dozen plays.) And, based on the conclusion of *Pope Bob* and *O Father*, Bill seems to be a big fan of them, too. They don't work for every novel but they might be just the ticket for yours.

50
WEEK NINE, DAY 1

BD: Reaching the Home Stretch

How about that! Can crack off 500 words each day ... day after day.

A novelist at work.

No sense wasting time here. Get back to your manuscript!

51
WEEK NINE, DAY 2

LWS: Good Knight, Look at You!

If these were medieval times your days as a squire—a knight-in-training—would quickly be coming to an end.

Over the past eight weeks you've practiced, refined, and discovered (in yourself) a lot of a novelist's skills.

Well done!

52
WEEK NINE, DAY 3

BD: On Letting Go

I don't know about medieval squires and knights but I have taught some young children how to ride a bike. My family's tradition was no training wheels but, instead, an adult huffing and puffing alongside the little trainee. Then, when it was apparent the child "had it," letting go.

Little Willie and I have let go.

53
WEEK NINE, DAY 4

LWS: In a Word

Huzzah!

54
WEEK NINE, DAY 5

BD: In Another Word

Whooooo-hooooo!

55
WEEK NINE, DAY 6

LWS: With the (Almost) Final Word

And here you are.

Just.

Like.

That.

Beginning.

Middle.

End.

Write today's word count. Finish your novel. Take tomorrow off. And the next day, too, if you like. Then, before you do anything with the manuscript (except back it up), return here for a little chat.

56
MONTHS LATER

Down the Road

Bill here. Again, congratulations to you!

I want to publically thank Little Willie for all his help. I haven't been in touch with him over the past few days and he hasn't been in touch with me, which—psychologically speaking—is probably a very good thing.

Now, with your novel completed (backed up and stored in at least two separate geographic locations), it's time for:

1. The surprise ending.
2. One more hard part.

The surprise ending that *is* one more hard part.

It's in your best interest to put aside your novel for four or five months before you reread it. In the meantime, start on your next novel.

Once you're quite a ways into Number 2, take a look at Number 1. You'll notice the second is a lot better than the first. You'll always love your first novel in a special way just because it *was* your first but ...

Well, no one wants to call a baby ugly but ... .

The advantage of waiting many months before rereading your first novel (or, heaven forbid, having someone else take a look at it) is you'll be much more objective about it. That's especially so if you're already well into Number 2 because— it will be readily apparent—you're doing a much better job on the second one.

Of course you are.

And the only way you could get to that point is by writing Number 1. (By getting *that* book out of the way.)

Your first novel wasn't the height of your novel-writing career or ability. It was a stepping stone to greater skills and to the sure knowledge that you *can* write a novel. A complete novel. Now you can write an even better novel.

And, if you like, an even longer novel.

Now there's no reason to stick to the nine-week formula but I do highly recommend you maintain a rigid daily word count. (A reasonable, workable, daily word count.) And that you take off one day a week.

Before I leave you, I want to say a few things about publishing. Perhaps as you wrote Novel 1 you wondered about getting an agent and getting your book published. (Yeah, "perhaps.") And, you thought, if that didn't happen there was always self-publishing, in a hard-copy or e-book format.

Self-publishing doesn't have the stigma it did even at the beginning of this century, but there are still some individuals and companies that take advantage of new writers. Beware! Check to see what the latest scams are. But ... know that some very fine writers now also self-publish or only self-publish.

Still ... .

Don't rush to get Novel 1 out there until you've completed Novel 2 and beyond. Like that first attempt at baking bread, some things are best not shared with anyone but a few trusted and supportive loved ones.

But enough of all this!

I leave you with one bit of advice I try to follow daily. Keep writing, dear novelist! Keep writing!

—Bill

Appendix: Sample Chapters

BD: Which, to be honest, seem like a bunch of commercials.

LWS: Which, to be honest, they are.

BD. Too much honesty is the worst policy.

LWS: First helpful advice you've given in the whole bloody book.

BD: How 'bout I just throw you back into a dresser drawer?

LWS: Please do.

O Father

The one I wrote for the 3-Day Novel Contest back in 1990. (Boy, am I old.)

Chapter 1

She snuggled in closer to me as the rain continued to tap against the car. We had been parked on the side of the road for twenty minutes and the windows were starting to steam up. The rain, the steam, and the lack of streetlights on that September 1990 evening made it seem like we were the only people in the world. I gave her a squeeze and then brushed my fingers through her fine blond hair. She sighed a little and a part of me wanted that moment to last forever. A big part of me. Then she turned her perfect face to look up at me and her blue eyes signaled trouble. "I gotta go potty," she said. "Real bad."

Jim Rockford never had this problem. I'm sure of it. I've watched every episode of *The Rockford Files* about a million times and old Jimbo is never out on a stakeout with someone who says, "I gotta go potty. Real bad."

But then Jim Rockford doesn't have a three-year-old daughter. And if he did, he sure wouldn't be stupid enough to take her with him when he was out tailing somebody.

"Poop or potty?" I asked, using that fine distinction parents make between defecating and urinating.

"Potty!" she said sitting up straight and looking around, as if maybe I had installed a toilet in my 1981 Malibu.

"You sure?" I pressed, knowing full well she was sure all right.

"I gotta go apple juice!"

I had her cousin to thank for that little term. He was the

122

one we were tailing. Sort of just for fun and sort of for this stupid course I was taking on how to be a private investigator.

By then my darling, full-bladdered daughter Carla was fidgeting so much she was in danger of banging her head on the roof of the car.

"I have to mail in my homework tomorrow," I said. "I have to follow somebody for at least three hours. We've only been doing this for ... " I squinted at my watch, "twenty minutes."

"It's coming out!"

Hell.

I opened my door and pulled her out behind me. The cute tapping of the rain wasn't so cute anymore. We were on a residential street in the Seattle suburb of Mountlake Terrace, a blue-collar town not known for anything.

I felt at home here.

A ten-foot hedge—a wild clump of bushes—surrounded the house we were parked in front of and I pulled her in there. We both got drenched and I wondered if maybe she wouldn't have stayed a lot drier if she'd just remained in the car and peed her pants.

But then that's probably some kind of trauma for a kid. I mean, once they're out of diapers and all that. Big setback psychologically. Not really great for the Malibu's front seat, either.

The bushes were like a mini-forest.

"Pee!" I commanded her.

She looked at me as if I were crazy, but then I'd grown accustomed to that over the past two and a half years.

"Pull down your pants and your underpants," I explained, "then kind of squat down and do it."

This would be a lot easier if you were a boy, I thought, wondering if that made me a sexist pig or a realist.

She tried to squat and fell on her can. She yelped and I laughed as I helped her get back up. She laughed too and we both pulled wet dead leaves off her hiney.

"Now you know why bears don't go poop in the woods," I said.

"Huh?"

"They never go. That's what makes them growl all the time."

"What bear?" She looked around.

"The only thing bare around here is your rump. Come on. Hurry up."

I held her hands and she tried squatting again. Nothing. A minute passed.

"Hurry up," I said.

Nothing. Another minute.

"Come on, honey. Go potty."

Maybe she couldn't go because we were out in the dark in the rain in the middle of some bushes. Maybe she went when we were laughing. Maybe a million things. What did I know about any of this? I knew I didn't want to get back in the car and then hear, "I gotta go potty."

"It's now or never, honey," I warned her. "Do it for Daddy. Come on, honey. Do it for Daddy."

The metallic click sounded very substantial. Expensive even. Not like somebody crushing a beer can or snicking a door shut. Like ... like ...

Holy Christ, Jimbo! Like a gun!

"Freeze. Police," a man's voice said, and then I was blind.

"Oh, dear God, crap!" said one part of my brain, the emotional part. "Must be one of those halogen light bulb flashlights," the logical side responded.

Neither was much help. Fortunately my body obeyed. I froze.

Unfortunately Carla's body didn't. She started to go potty. On my right shoe.

"You okay, kid?" he asked.

She smiled into the bright light. "Bears don't go poop in

the bushes," she said.

"This is my daughter," I said.

"Uh-huh."

"And ... " I forced a laugh. "... she was caught a little short. Kids." I shrugged.

"Uh-huh."

"So you see there's nothing really going on here and ... "

"Can you get dressed by yourself, little girl?"

She shot the cop a look and said, "Since I was two!" She proved it and then we stood side by side facing him.

"Head for the street," he instructed and gestured with the light, pointing it over our heads for an instant as if we might have forgotten which way it was to the road.

"No problem, officer," I said. Practically sang.

It was maybe thirty feet back out to our car. "Okay, Mr. 'Do it for Daddy,' hug the front fender."

This probably would have seemed even more frightening if I hadn't done it before. Or maybe it would have seemed less frightening. I'm sure this wouldn't have been the same if I hadn't done it before. I had. Assumed the position.

It's not the kind of thing you tend to forget like returning a library book or getting your oil changed or paying the utility bill. Assuming the position is a memorable experience. Even the second time around.

It was still raining. I wanted to wipe my face off but I didn't. He patted me down, much more thoroughly than anyone ever patted down Jim Rockford. On camera, anyway.

"Leave my daddy alone," Carla said, and I was very proud of her. "Butt head," she added.

"Carla, honey, be nice to the police officer," I turned my head and instructed her. Then I realized she might not believe he really was a cop because he wasn't wearing a uniform. He had on jeans and a leather jacket that was really soaked.

At least he got to wipe his face off when he wanted to.

Then, too, maybe it was a good thing she had called him only a "butt head." Her vocabulary had really increased since Frankie—excuse me—Frank moved in.

"Butt head," she repeated. "Poop for brains."

She smacked him one on the leg and he gave a kick. "Back off," he said.

"Hey," I said, and almost turned around. Almost took my hands off the front of the Malibu. Almost resisted arrest.

Could I see your badge?" I asked.

"No.

"Let's see the badge!"

My hands were still on the car.

"Do you see the gun?"

He had a point. He also had handcuffs. He let me wear them. Then he marched me back up the street a couple of houses to a big Ford parked behind my car. It was an unmarked police car.

I wondered if I could get extra credit in P.I. school for this little experience. I wondered if Frankie had driven off while I was being harassed by this butt head.

He leaned me against the hood of the car—face down—and then opened the passenger door, reached in and pulled out the microphone. He had my wallet. I must have been distracted when his other hand was rummaging around in my private parts.

He mumbled some macho-sounding stuff into the microphone. Suddenly sirens were whooping in from all over the place. But the cars—marked and unmarked—blew by us and stopped up the street. All I caught from his mumbo-jumbo was "wants and warrants" and then "Fitzpatrick, Kevin M.," and my birth date and address and the license plate number on the Malibu.

This was not good.

I mean, it wasn't as if I had some unpaid parking tickets. Who got parking tickets in Mountlake Terrace? We didn't even have one parking meter. Teenagers were more likely to be cited for riding their horses on the wrong side of the street.

I don't have any tickets but I'm sort of on parole.

Okay, I'm really on parole, but only for two more years. That's why this was not so good.

The dispatcher garbled out some other stuff.

"No computers in the cars yet, huh?" I asked, hoping to establish some kind of a relationship here.

"Shut the hell up."

Carla was clinging to my right leg. I was willing to bet that, psychologically speaking, it would have been much better for her if I had just let her wet her pants.

The police officer and the dispatcher squawked at each other some more and then he was done there and he turned his full attention to me.

"Tough guy, huh?" he asked.

"No, sir."

He pulled me up and spun me around. He was maybe three or four inches taller than I am. I'm two inches short of six feet. That meant a lot more to me when I was in high school. Now, at thirty-eight, it doesn't seem to matter too much.

He also looked a couple years older than I am. That would make him forty. I smiled.

"What's so funny?"

"Nothing, sir."

"I don't think I'd be laughing if I was in your shoes."

"Yes, sir."

Carla was crying into my pants.

"I'm taking this class," I explained, "and I was supposed to follow somebody and so I was following my nephew. Well, partly for the class and partly because we had this fight this morning and I was feeling kind of bad about that and I wanted to tell him ..."

"You beatin' up your nephew?"

"No, sir! I mean we had a disagreement. We exchanged

words."

"You want to be a private investigator?" he asked, going to an earlier point in my explanation. He said it the way you would say "scrub toilets" or "kick puppies." The way most people would say "kick puppies." Not this guy. He might kind of like that.

"No, sir," I said. "I want to be a writer."

"A rider?"

"A writer. Write stuff."

He shook his head. "So why aren't you in writing school?"

"I've been to writing school."

The radio shouted out a few more unintelligible things.

"Great," he said. "From now on, your kid has to take a leak, you make sure she does it inside, okay?"

"Yes, sir."

He spun me back around and started to undo the cuffs when more radio squawks made him stop. He cussed a little bit, almost under his breath, and then pushed me back toward my car.

"Hey," I said, waving my arms a little to remind him he forgot to take off the handcuffs.

"Shut up."

Carla was hanging on to my pocket as she walked along beside me. After we passed the Malibu I noticed a bunch of other cars parked in front of the house Frankie had gone into. Fords.

One was in the driveway. It was painted gray with a Mountlake Terrace Police sticker on the front doors and a rack of lights and siren up top. Francis Michael Fitzpatrick was in the back seat.

* * *

Pope Bob

What if ... the first American pope is an alcoholic? Written in the early 1990s.

Chapter 1

His Holiness, Pope Leo XVII, Vicar of Christ, Bishop of Rome and Servant of the Servants of God, opened his eyes and wondered if he was going to throw up.

He thought he might. So was it better to get out of bed and head for the bathroom or stay motionless and pray for death?

His eyes swept the room. It was dawn. Where was he? Never mind what city or what country, what continent was he on?

He closed his eyes as his stomach churned.

North America. Canada. Calgary, Alberta. No. Vancouver, British Columbia. Last night had been the big Mass at BC Place Stadium. Today he would be flying home. Well, flying back to the Vatican anyway. Another visit completed. Thank God.

It was a prayer.

"The pontiff," he said out loud to himself, "has to pee."

He opened his eyes again and turned his head toward the bed table on his left. "Too fast," he mumbled and the pain made him wince. The clock said 5:14. The empty bottle of Johnnie Walker Black said something else.

"Today, Lord," he prayed, "I'm not going to drink. I'm not going to drink. I'm not going to drink."

Both he and God knew he was lying.

Maybe there was a swallow or two left in the bottle. A little hair of the dog to take care of his pounding head. He sat up on one elbow. Nope. That puppy was dead.

He tried to remember what had happened the previous day. The kid in the cowboy hat had come up to him and ...

No. That was Calgary. The day before yesterday. It had been the high point of the trip for him. A six-year-old boy decked out in Western gear strode right up to him, stuck out his hand, and said, "Hiya, Pope!"

Cardinals, bishops, governors, judges and a famous Canadian actor were mortified. The kid was supposed to say "Welcome to Calgary, Your Holiness."

Hiya, Pope!

Even now it made him smile. Someone who treated him like a real, live person instead of the Successor of Peter.

"Nice hat," Pope Leo had commented and the kid answered, "Better'n yours." The child was right. The Holy Father was wearing a white zucchetto, the small skull cap that fit on the back of his head.

"Don't want to trade, huh?" the pope had asked the boy.

"A Stetson for a beanie?" he had scoffed and the dignitaries had blanched. "I'm not stupid."

Pope Leo ended up giving the boy the zucchetto. No strings attached. The youngster mumbled a hasty "thank you" when his mother pointedly cleared her throat but it was obvious he didn't think it was any great prize.

"You're right, kid," Pope Leo now whispered to himself as he swung his legs over the edge of the bed and sat up all the way.

"I won't throw up. I won't throw up. I won't throw up," he chanted softly and waited for his stomach to settle back down. "Wrong again," he muttered. He stood quickly and hurried to the bathroom. He emerged five minutes later trembling and pale but feeling a little better.

Fresh air. That was what he needed. A nice walk. He thought about what that would entail. Dozens of guards, both his own and those provided by the Canadian government. And clerics all over the place. Surrounding him. Oh, my yes, that would be relaxing and refreshing.

He checked the clock. How long until that gentle, insistent tapping on his door? "Your Holiness. Your Holiness? Your Holiness!"

Maybe forty-five minutes. A forty-five minute walk just before dawn. Alone. It sounded so good. Heavenly. If he only had some time to himself he was sure he wouldn't be drinking so much. It was just the stress.

He looked at the clothes that had been laid out for him. White cassock and all. Not the best for traveling incognito.

He opened the bedroom door a crack. A rectory. That was where he was. Holy Rosary Cathedral rectory. He glanced down the long hallway. It was empty but he could hear voices coming from around a corner. Two guards talking about marathons and split times.

Hello, what was this? God is good. On a straight-backed chair next to his door were a pair of old sweat pants, a hooded sweat shirt and a pair of running shoes. One of his protectors must have been out getting his morning exercise and temporarily dumped them there.

Pope Leo snatched the items, pulled back into the bedroom and quietly shut the door. "It's not stealing," he said. "I'm merely borrowing."

They were all too big for him but he didn't care. He slipped into them and strapped on his wristwatch. Forty-five minutes of heaven.

Leo flipped up the hood, pulled the drawstring a bit so that his face was hidden and stepped out into the hall. He quickly walked away from the voices. A rectory this big had to have a back staircase, didn't it?

"Bingo!" the pope whispered when he found it. He descended into the kitchen. A cook glanced at him, figuring it was a member of the pope's guard. A member of the guard sitting at a table looked up from a newspaper and assumed it was one of the local priests dressed in civvies. He nodded toward each, his face obscured by the large hood.

He opened the back door and stepped out on the porch. A Mountie was there but he was looking out, not in. "Morning," the pope said and the Mountie grunted without turning his head.

He walked down the stairs, across the back yard and out a gate. No one screamed. No one ran after him. He was free.

* * *

Mildred Nudge:
A Widower's Tale

Written in the winter of 2014, one year after my wife, Monica, died.

Jack Tobit assumed it was the onions. That was the problem. Not the pepperoni, sausage, mushrooms, black olives, or green peppers. Not the chocolate birthday cake.

Should have picked them off.

All right, should have skipped the late-night snack of cold, leftover pizza. And cake.

He sat in the dark on his side of the bed and burped softly.

Onions.

You turn sixty, he thought, *you got to start wising up.*

Sixty.

Already.

He could hear his wife breathing gently on her side of the bed and was glad his latest little acid-reflux wake-up call hadn't disturbed her.

He glanced at the clock on his nightstand—three one seven—and was considering how many antacid tablets he should take when he heard the television downstairs in the living room. Voice, voice, voice, canned laughter. Voice, voice, voice, canned laughter.

The syncopation of the situation comedy.

He walked to the hallway landing and looked down. A gray light. Andy Taylor talking to Barney Fife. Now he could hear the words. Line, line, line, laughter.

Who had … ?

Was one of the girls home?

"Hey," he whispered loudly. Shouted softly?

"Yeah?" a voice answered.

Kelly or Rachel? One a thirty-three-year-old mother of three, the other two years younger and engaged to be married next summer. Both girls living in the area. Both with house keys. Neither likely to stop by in the middle of the night.

Unless something was wrong.

"What's wrong?" Jack asked as he walked down the stairs.

"What?"

"Why are you here?"

"Here?"

He still couldn't tell which one it was. She was sitting in a high-backed winged chair that faced the TV and opposite the stairway.

He heard Opie Taylor's voice and looked at the screen. A real oldie. In black and white. "This is one of my favorites," he said, standing next to the chair.

"I know," she said. "We used to watch it in the rec room on that plastic portable with the broken antenna."

He nodded. "Yeah." He hadn't thought about that room or that television set in more than forty years. He frowned. How did she … ?

He turned to his left and looked down.

"What the … !"

A small, slender, white woman in her late seventies or early eighties. Feet up on the ottoman. Dark blue running shoes. Light blue sweatshirt and sweatpants. The dressy kind. Black hair. Straight. Short. Bangs. Cut like Imogene Coca's. Or Hetty's on *NCIS: Los Angeles*. Or Moe's of Three Stooges fame. A what do you call it? Rachel had one when she was in the first grade. Pixie?

A dream!

Of course.

He was having a dream.

Sleeping restlessly because of that stupid pizza. That stupid onion on that stupid "everything" pizza.

"Should've picked them off," Jack said.

"What I thought," she said, not taking her eyes off the show.

"What?"

"What?" she answered.

"What are you talking about?" he asked.

"Onions," she said. "What are you talking about?"

"This is a weird dream," he said.

"Mmm," she answered.

"You're kind of Imogene, Hetty, Moe," he said.

"Imogene Coca? How old *are* you anyway?"

So that was it!

"So that's it," he said to her. "This is a 'late-night-pizza and I-feel-old' kind of dream."

"You *are* old," she said matter-of-factly.

"Only sixty."

"Only old people say 'only sixty'," she said.

She had a point.

"It used to be old," he said.

"They say that, too."

He felt his defenses stir.

"Well, how old are *you*?" he asked.

She looked up at him for the first time.

"In earth years?" she said and he grinned. Delighted.

Yes! He couldn't wait to tell Ann about his dream. He loved it when it was some bizarre scene and he could say, "And *then* it got weird."

* * *

The World's Funniest Atheist

I liked the idea of an atheist suddenly being given the "gift of faith" and absolutely not wanting it. I wrote this in 2012.

Chapter 1

"No!" Bang.

"No!" Bang.

"No!" Bang.

"No!" Bang.

"No! No! No!" Bang, bang, bang, h-o-o-o-o-o-nk!

Saul McNeil had his car window down and could hear the kids in the next car laughing at him as he screamed and slammed his hands against the steering wheel. "No, no, no, no, no," one of them mimicked. The driver laid on the horn and the other teens erupted in howls of laughter.

"Little jerks," Saul shouted at them.

"Old age road rage," one shot back.

Old? he thought.

"Who you calling old!" he asked.

More laughter.

Forget it, he thought. Try telling a sixteen-year-old that forty-five isn't old. Trying telling a sixteen-year-old anything. He assumed they were sixteen. They sounded like it. Punks. But he couldn't see them. His world was very bright and very dark, and light hurt and sound hurt, and—oh, Lord—here it came.

Saul fumbled with his door lock, opened the door, leaned out quickly and—forgetting about his seat belt— threw up half on the road and half on himself.

"Got it!" one of the kids yelled and the others cheered.

"Go to hell!" Saul shouted, wiping off his mouth and

136

spitting out the doorway.

He could hear the traffic starting to move again. The teens' car inched forward and the driver behind him honked.

Saul slammed his door shut and stared straight ahead. Light, dark, and weird shards of color. That was how he had described it to a doctor one time. The physician had only nodded, said "Mmm hmm" and launched into a mini-lesson on migraine headaches. Hard to say for sure what causes them. Hard to find the best remedy for an individual who experiences them. Easy to charge for the office visit that had told him practically nothing.

"Move!" the driver behind Saul shouted.

"Drop dead!" he yelled back.

Saul heard a door open. A pickup? Then heavy boots heading his way. In a hurry.

"What did you ... ?" the voice began.

"Get back in the truck," another man ordered. A voice that was used to telling people what to do and having them do it.

"Have you been drinking, sir?" the voice asked Saul.

"What?" He tried to put the colorful shards of reality back into a coherent whole. A badge. A gun belt.

"No," he said.

"Drugs?"

"No," Saul said.

"So what's going on?" the officer asked.

"Headache."

"You're hung over?"

"Migraine."

"Do you need medical assistance, sir?"

"What? No. Just some place quiet and dark for a while."

This would have to be June 21, the first day of summer and the longest day of the year. Now about four in the afternoon, there were still more than five hours of daylight.

"Can you operate your vehicle, sir?"

"Sure." He faced front and squinted.

"Uh-huh. How many fingers am I holding up, sir?"

He turned to his left. "Three."

"I don't have my hand up, sir."

"Then how am I supposed to know how many fingers you're holding up? Or holding down, I guess."

"Uh-huh," the officer said. "Someone else is going to have to move your car, sir. We can't have you blocking traffic."

"I'll do it," an old guy shouted. How do I know he's old? Saul thought. By the sound of that voice the man had to be at least in his mid-seventies. You're in your mid-forties then mid-seventies is old. You're in your mid-teens and mid-forties is old. It's all relative, he decided.

"You got this, Reb?" he heard the officer ask the old man.

"Sure."

"Come on out, sir." Saul heard the car door open. "We're going to put you in the passenger seat and the Reb here will get your car out of the way, okay?"

"Sure."

"He said he needs some place dark and quiet," the officer said.

"I got that," the old man said.

"Hell," Saul muttered as they moved him.

"Those headaches are hell," Reb agreed.

"Yeah," Saul said, knowing that was the least of his problems.

* * *

My Great-grandfather
Turns 12 Today

I wanted to write another novel for kids and I wanted something with time travel. This was first published in 2010.

Chapter 1

"Hurry up, Michael, we're going to be late!" my father yelled up the stairs at me.

Maybe Michael doesn't even want to go, I thought. Did that ever occur to you? Maybe Michael has better things to do on his twelfth birthday than ride all the way to Fair Brook and be around a bunch of old people who smell like they wet their pants.

Most of them don't even wear pants, I corrected myself. They just sit around or lie around in those stupid gowns and robes and they drool and cough.

Happy birthday, dear Michael. Happy birthday to me.

I stared out the window. It was raining really hard. There was some lightning and thunder.

"Mom says you can open one present before we go!" Dad shouted up at me. Present? All right!

I found my jacket. For some reason my brother had stuffed it under my bed. Probably I had accidentally left it on "his" side of the room and so he had crammed it under there. That was so typical.

"Michael!"

I was heading downstairs when I heard that same stupid brother ask, "How come he gets to open a present now?"

"Just one," my mom said. "We're opening the rest of them at Fair Brook."

That'll be fun, I thought. We can pass them around and let everyone slobber on them.

"But we're not supposed to open presents until after the cake," he said. "That the way we always do it."

For a guy who was only fourteen, Robert was a real pain when it came to explaining how it had to be done. He always knew how everything had to be done. And he was always ready to tell the rest of us.

"Get a grip," David said. That was my other older brother. He was sixteen and had just gotten his driver's license and his letter jacket for track. David was madly in love with ... David. But at least most of the time he was on my side. That was mainly because he knew it really bugged Robert.

"How far to Fair Brook?" he asked my dad.

As if we hadn't been there a billion times.

"About thirty-five miles," Dad said.

David looked at his watch. "We should get going," he said.

Oh, okay, Dad Junior.

"He only gets to open a small present, huh?" Robert asked.

"I get to pick," I said, thinking: Roll on out that brand new bike!

"Here." Mom handed me a shopping bag that wasn't very heavy.

"I guess there's not a bicycle in here, huh?" I asked and she laughed as if I had made a joke.

"We figured you can have David's old bike," Dad said.

David's old bike! That piece of junk?

"Not have," David corrected them. "I said he could buy it from me. Cheap."

Talk about cheap.

"How much?" I asked.

"We'll discuss that later," Dad said. "We've got to get going."

"So open one!" That was my little sister Sarah who was almost nine. She had just finished the third grade. She was all right for short periods of time.

"You want me to go warm up the car?" David asked my dad.

In the middle of June? It was raining not snowing.

"I think it'll be okay," Dad said.

"So is he gonna open a stupid present or what?" Robert whined. "I don't want to waste all my Saturday at that place."

Dad didn't exactly growl but when he exhaled there was something there that said, "Watch out!"

"I mean," Robert quickly added, "I have a few other things I have to do later today and so I think we should get going."

"So open one," Sarah said again.

I looked in the bag. There were four or five packages inside. All in "Happy Birthday" wrapping paper. "What's my main one?" I asked Mom.

"No fair," Robert said. "On my birthday I had to wait until …"

"This one." Mom reached in and pulled out the smallest package. It was about five inches long, an inch and a half wide, and an inch and a half deep. She handed it to me. It was heavy.

"Probably a harmonica," David said.

I hate that! I hate when people guess what's in a wrapped-up present and then they're right and they say, "I told you so."

"Nope," Dad said.

"It's small," I said to Robert. "You said it would be okay if I opened a small one."

"Shut up."

"Boys," my mom said.

He started it, I thought.

"Probably a pocket knife," David said. I tore open the

paper before he could make another guess. I was already too late. "Told you," he said, sounding smug.

It was one of those Swiss Army knives. The red ones. The kind that have a bunch of stuff beside blades. A screwdriver and tweezers and toothpick and saw and leather punch and can opener and bunch of other stuff.

"Cool," I said and then remembered to add, "Thank you."

Dad nodded and Mom gave me a little hug.

"Can I take it with me?" I asked.

"Sure," Dad said. "I know Great-grandpa would love to see it."

That brought me back to reality. Dad's grandpa. My great-grandpa. That's who we were going to see at Fair Brook. He and I have the same birthday: June 21. He was eighty-eight when I was born in 1974. I never got to have a birthday all to myself.

Today I turned twelve. That made him one hundred. The whole family—grandparents and aunts and uncles and cousins—were getting together to celebrate. They were getting together for Great-grandpa, not for me.

I wondered if he would even be awake for any of it.

"Grandpa told me Great-grandpa wants to talk to you," Dad said to me.

"Gee, that'll be fun," Robert said and then wrapped his lips around his teeth and pretended he was trying to talk but he didn't have any teeth.

"Robert!" Mom said and he shut up. Then she went to the kitchen to get my birthday cake, some bags of chips, and some potato salad; and Dad, David, and Sarah headed for the car.

Robert gave me his "gummy" face again and whispered, "Probably wants to give you a great, big birthday kiss."

* * *

ABOUT THE AUTHOR

Bill Dodds—who's writing this himself but apparently it's supposed to be done in the third person — has been writing full-time since the Jimmy Carter administration. That is, 1978. Ten years at a newspaper and then freelance. Tons of articles and columns. Editor of two national magazines. Forty-plus books. Give or take. Fiction and non-fiction. For kids and grown-ups. (Bill has learned not to say "I write adult novels.") Bunch of awards. In a filing cabinet, somewhere.

More at BillDodds.com but, honestly, haven't you had enough of him to last a long while? You can email him at WFDodds@gmail.com and tell him just that.

Sorry. One more.
He still really loves to write
and wishes you the absolute best on your novel.

Look! A blank page.
No, shoot. Now it isn't blank.
Never mind.

Made in the USA
Lexington, KY
27 October 2019

56122541R00095